SCIENCE AND ENGINEERING POLICY SERIES

General Editors Sir Harrie Massey
Sir Frederick Dainton
The late Lord Jackson of Burnley

The New Scientists

Edited by David Fishlock

OXFORD UNIVERSITY PRESS 1971

Oxford University Press   *Ely House, London W.1*

Glasgow	Bombay
New York	Calcutta
Toronto	Madras
Melbourne	Karachi
Wellington	Lahore
Cape Town	Dacca
Salisbury	Kuala Lumpur
Ibadan	Singapore
Nairobi	Hong Kong
Dar es Salaam	Tokyo
Lusaka	
Addis Ababa	

Printed in Great Britain by
William Clowes & Sons Ltd.
London, Colchester and Beccles

Contents

Introduction
by David Fishlock, Financial Times   1

Hans Kronberger
by Sir Brian Flowers, F.R.S.   9

The authors   13

1   How the atom paid off
by Hans Kronberger, F.R.S.   16

2   Creativity and the central laboratory
by Duncan S. Davies, Imperial Chemical Industries   28

3   The synthesis of ideas
by D. T. N. Williamson, F.R.S., Molins Limited, London   38

4   Harwell changes course
by W. Marshall, Atomic Energy Research Establishment, Harwell   55

5   Defence research under pressure
by H. W. Pout, Admiralty Surface Weapons Establishment   71

6   Management science and government
by B. T. Price, Vickers Limited   82

Index   97

Introduction
By David Fishlock

There is some cause to think that in Britain, among other nations, much of science is now subject to the law of diminishing returns. For a nation whose future, industrially, depends in large measure on the creation of new technology, ahead of others, which it can license profitably to others with industrial ambitions, the suggestion is somewhat discouraging.

But is it true? Need it cost more and more in research and development to achieve less and less, or can we organize science to show a better return for an investment of roughly £1000 million a year? Those whose views are most frequently heard on the subject of the organization and management of research are, first, the academics, who cannot and should not be expected to make their primary purpose the pay-off from science; and, secondly, the elder statesmen of science, whether in boardrooms or departments of government. Between them, of course, these men must be accounted responsible for any short-comings in present-day policies and practices.

The new scientists affords a fresh point of view. Six relatively young research managers, still in their thirties and forties, were invited to present highly personal accounts of their own efforts to steer research into more productive channels. All but one, Dr. Kronberger, who died in September 1970, have important responsibilities for the management and direction of scientific resources in Britain today.

In the first chapter, Kronberger ('How the atom paid off') reviews briefly the creation of the atomic energy project, the most ambitious and fertile R and D programme ever launched in Britain, which provided the nation with a new kind of weapon—its original mission— and also a competitive new kind of power, from which Britain by 1980 will be drawing one-fourth of her needs. The project pioneered in Britain the assessment of R and D programmes on the basis of cost-effectiveness. A career spent with this programme since its inception taught Kronberger that most scientists 'prefer to work on urgent projects in need of solutions, rather than to provide solutions in search of applications'. Like other people, he found, they want to feel wanted, preferably indispensable, and tend to work better when complaining that there is 'no time to think'.

The atomic programme, with its heady excitement and manifold pressures, was just the kind of environment in which such minds flourished. What is more, with more projects to tackle than could comfortably be accommodated, the perennial R and D problem of how to stop projects no longer existed. Just offer a chance, Kronberger found, to start a new project and the one that had outlived its value or prospects would soon be shed. So much, then, for the idea that scientists tend to resist change.

So strong an organization was built up in this way that one might think that it has gone too far, isolating itself by its own excellence from the new industry it set out to create, which in turn grows supine and fails to sieze its chances. But industry itself is not immune to this problem, as Chapter 2 makes plain. Here Davies ('Creativity and the central laboratory') shows how a company can deliberately encourage ideas, 'ideas being a product that is preferable to more of the orthodox goods for sale'. But one big hazard for centralized research in a decentralized organization is the ease with which it can become an ivory tower, pursuing its goals oblivious—even in defiance—of commercial objectives. The risk of isolation is heightened in a company—such as Davies's—with established research groups in each of its product divisions, for ideas from the centre may then be resented as 'not invented here', the N.I.H. factor.

None the less, 'We have a suspicion', writes Davies, 'that orthodox educational procedures and business environments sometimes either stifle [the scientists'] originality or deflect their talents into more conventional, logical channels.' The successful central laboratory can salvage these commercially valuable assets, he suggests, by providing inventors and discoverers—the 'artists' of industry—with an environment that encourages the unusual idea or invention. But Davies warns: 'Unless the central laboratory is identifiably different from business-group research teams, and pursues extra and ultimately profitable objectives, it has no purpose. Unless it is compatible with them it has no results.'

Where Davies writes from a research-conscious industry, Williamson ('The synthesis of ideas') does not; but their themes are in harmony. Individuals, not organizations, are the most prolific source of ideas. Anyone who attempts to employ creativity more productively must be prepared to accommodate the 'cranky individualist, motivated more by the intellectual excitement of the process than by the possible rewards . . .' But Britain needs first to find and encourage a great many more people with creative talent, and a fundamental obstacle here is her educational system for engineers, which totally fails to develop the synthesis approach to ideas for new products.

Like Davies, he contends that the development of a new engineering project is incomplete until the new product is in production. It is precisely the phase of development immediately preceding production that incurs the greatest expense. Yet at this difficult and crucial point in its gestation the project is frequently transferred to others, sometimes less capable, but invariably, for obvious reasons, less eager to see it succeed than those whose creation it was. This dichotomy, suggests Williamson, is probably the most damaging factor it is possible to have in an engineering company. Usually the damage comes to light only indirectly, in the muted performance of the manufacturer and, ultimately, the nation. But one well-publicized consequence of such a dichotomy was the initial failure in 1969 of the high-speed, high-pressure turbines designed specially for the *Queen Elizabeth 2*, where long before the project's completion the design team had been disbanded.

At first sight, the Williamson case seems irreconcilable with that argued by Marshall ('Harwell changes course'), who describes how one of Europe's largest and most famous laboratories has turned from its original nuclear mission to a much broader programme of work 'in support of industrial objectives'. Many industrial research directors in Britain are convinced that government laboratories have no part to play in commercial research beyond their original brief, usually in the ill-defined area of 'basic' research, standards, and suchlike. One of the first moves made by Harwell was to canvass industry's views. The response was entirely unambiguous. 'Industry simply did not want us', writes Marshall, 'and most people sought strongly to discourage us.' It was believed that if the 'redundant' laboratories were closed, industry would absorb their skills, and a direct transfer of technology would thereby take place. The national research budget could then be used to subsidize the scientists' presence in industry.

Far from being deterred by industry's attitude, Harwell responded by devising a scheme of collaboration not unlike that used—

manifestly successfully—by the big United States sponsored research organizations such as Battelle. Whereas in the past the government laboratories have been accustomed to making their results in all but defence research freely available (with discouragingly few takers in, for example, engineering), Harwell today in non-nuclear research cheerfully flouts this tradition. Its groups engage in projects with specific companies, with the ruthless exclusion of rivals, even sharing the cost—and the risk. Aptly, the Harwell scientists dubbed it the 'principle of maximum unfairness'. The commercial collaborator gains access to the facilities of an exceptionally well-equipped and creative national laboratory, whose staff in turn are placed more closely in touch with new product development than, for some years past, they have been accustomed to, even in their nuclear role.

The vigour with which many government scientists at Harwell and elsewhere plied their new trade of sponsored research, and the success of their salesmanship, convinced the Ministry of Technology that herein lay a way of harnessing Britain's civil research facilities more effectively to commercial advantage. In January 1970 the Labour Government proposed a merger of ten national laboratories and the National Research Development Corporation, agency of commercial exploitation for many of the inventions made with public funds in these laboratories, universities, and elsewhere.

By research standards the proposed British Research and Development Corporation[1] would have been a big body, for its components spend around £70 million a year, and have capital assets of the same order. (For comparison, I.C.I. has a research and development budget of around £35 million; Battelle, the biggest American contract research company, an income of about £50 million.) While the core of its expertise, initially, would be nuclear, the corporation would start life with groups of international standing in, for example, standards and ship research, metallurgy, and hydraulic engineering. The idea was not entirely novel, for such a proposal had been advanced in the United States, which also faces the prospect of surplus research capacity in, especially, its national nuclear laboratories. But no American national laboratory has yet made the crucial experiment of applying the 'principle of maximum unfairness'; of attempting—and maintaining—exclusivity in its commercial dealings.

There is, however, one basic difference between the two nations. Unlike American industrial firms, very few British companies have research resources comparable with the national laboratories. The

United States, racked by social rather than economic stresses, has a desperate need to apply its technology to such problems as finding counter-measures to pollution, crime, drug addiction, and social disorder. Britain, meanwhile, urgently needs new technology that she can turn into cash. Success in this quarter, it is true, could easily heighten the social strains, but by placing the project with a national centre the government could ensure that it would be approached with this risk in mind. A solution would be attempted with a view both to economic return and social advantage. Such a project might aim at halving the present-day cost of digging tunnels—a neglected technology—which would immediately make it attractive to put much of our transport and urban facilities underground.

Three sources of income were envisaged for the research corporation. The government would provide a direct grant to cover basic research of the kind the government of any industrially ambitious nation needs to do. By this means, new technology is created, standards are set, and the government maintains a source of expert advice independent of purely commercial interest. In the early years this part of its work would inevitably have a big nuclear bias. The second course would be other government departments, which at present must cajole the Department of Trade to do work at its own expense. It would be 'a healthy discipline', the proposal argued, if other government departments paid directly for the research they sponsored. The third source of income would be private industry, with cash sometimes solicited on a risk-sharing basis, sometimes on other terms.

The alternative often advanced in industry and elsewhere, which is simply to close the 'redundant' laboratories, would have several disadvantages. The most obvious, from the national standpoint, as the *Financial Times* pointed out in a leader discussing the government's proposal,[2] are:

(1) It would involve the dispersal of research groups of, often, international standing;
(2) Those industries least likely at present to attract good scientists would be those—such as heavy engineering—most urgently in need of their services;
(3) The Government itself might lose a valuable source of advice independent of the commercial interest.

Pout ('Defence research under pressure') takes up this last point. The defence laboratories, which are excluded from the proposed research corporation, are engaged in R and D in a field where the 'cost-effective' approach is fairly novel. Defence, he points out, 'is not an activity to which accounting conventions and normal financial judgements can be applied'. None the less, it is one where the government, as never before, now seeks value for money. 'Much more than in the past, the likely performance, costs, and programme of military equipment are closely scrutinized, and the possibilities of collaborating with other countries, and of foreign purchases, are taken into account.'

As with civil research, many will argue that the cash should be spent in industrial centres. In fact, over half of Britain's defence R and D already is. But the rest, £109 million in 1968–9, is spent in maintaining government research of a sufficient calibre to evaluate the competition (the enemy's strength), decide what needs to be done, at what price, and assess the results. Like Williamson, Pout points out serious weaknesses in Britain's approach to educating people of a calibre capable of so exacting a task.

Omission of the defence laboratories, including the Atomic Weapons Research Establishment, from plans for the merger of research, has provoked criticism on the ground that it excludes from the proposed corporation much valuable expertise, in electronics especially. But the primary role of a defence laboratory is to ensure that the nation is keeping abreast of competition in weapons technology. As the more research-conscious portions of industry know well, there is no better way of keeping abreast of the competition than by the maintenance of research staff skilled in the technologies of a particular organization, and thus equipped above all to recognize the significance for its employers of advances elsewhere. In defence still more than in commerce the need is self-evident for a high level of security in what, after all, is a very sophisticated brand of espionage. This applies no less to establishments like the Chemical and Biological Research Establishments and the Atomic Weapons Research Establishment, whose primary role is to observe progress elsewhere, than to those whose primary role is to create new weapons.

Defence research, however, has produced an application of the scientific method in policy making that civil authorities are beginning to acknowledge has immensely productive possibilities. Management science, the term chosen by Price ('Management science and government'), embraces an inter-disciplinary approach to long-range planning in which operational research, econometrics, systems analysis, and social science all play their part. 'The great opportunity offered by management science is the creation of a bridge between the two professions, driven apart during the last hundred years by increasing specialization.' Price offers examples culled from his experience both as the director of a defence establishment, and latterly in a department, Transport, where because every customer tends to regard himself as an expert decisions are exposed to unusually ruthless public appraisal.

Technology assessment

The final chapter is highly relevant to the theme of this book—more productive research—for another reason. 'Whether rightly or wrongly', began a recent report of the American Academy of Sciences, 'the belief is now widely held that the continuation of certain technological trends would pose grave dangers for the future of man, and indeed that ill-considered exploitation has already contributed to some of the most urgent of our contemporary problems.'[3] Even among those who readily concede that technology has been a great boon to mankind, the report continued, 'there has emerged a great strain of scepticism towards proposals and projects that, in an earlier day, might have been hailed as the very symbols of human progress'.

Increasingly, technological decisions impinge on society at large. The United States Committee (under Dr. Harvey Brooks, the President's science adviser-at-large) that wrote this report, even defined technology as 'nothing more than a systematic way of altering the environment'. Who decides, however, whether the net result of an alteration will be to the benefit of society as a whole, not of one fortunate faction only? Too often in the past a decision appears to have been reached on the basis not so much of a case carefully weighed by dispassionate parties, but of a commitment for reasons of political prestige, or solely for profit. In the future it could even work in reverse. The prevailing enthusiasm for conservation and countermeasures to pollution or related abuses could encourage politicians to initiate bans on the use of scientific advances on the most slender evidence, for the sake of political kudos.

The Brooks Committee concluded that there were in the United States almost no mechanisms for 'technology assessment' that were not self-assessment. Nuclear schemes are assessed by the body charged with both the promotion and the regulation of nuclear energy, the United States Atomic Energy Commission. The technical assessment of the supersonic transport is in the hands of the Federal Aviation Agency, a most decidedly interested party. Too often, processes of assessment ignore the broader social and environmental contexts in which their effects are felt. Too often, in calculating costs and benefits, they ascribe too little significance to keeping future options open. Too little attention and support is given to research and monitoring programmes calculated to minimize technological surprise.

The American report recommended a highly professional approach: a Technology Assessment Office at White House level, backed by a new technology assessment division of the National Science Foundation, with a $50 million budget to support contracts and make grants in pursuit of an objective assessment. Britain is no less urgently in need of an independent method of assessment, versed in all the techniques outlined in this book, but, in particular, in those of Chapter 6.

References

1. *Industrial research and development in government laboratories: a new organization for the seventies.* H.M.S.O. (1970).
2. Value from a national asset. *Financial Times*, p. 16 (16 January 1970).
3. American Academy of Science, Committee on Science and Astronautics. *Technology: processes of assessment and choice.* U.S. Government Printing Office (1969).

Hans Kronberger

By Sir Brian Flowers, F.R.S.

> . . . and if I laugh at any mortal thing
> 'Tis that I may not weep.
>
> *Don Juan.*

Byron, had he known him, might have written these words specially for Hans Kronberger, who died on 29 September 1970, a few weeks after completing Chapter 1 of this book. For if his friends ask themselves what it was Hans did that each of them remembers most vividly, the answer must surely be: 'He made us laugh.' Yet it is mercifully difficult for most of us to imagine the mounting weight of personal tragedy he carried. He had the rare gift of always finding something, somewhere, to stimulate our interest and laughter.

It was in the early days of the Atomic Energy Research Establishment at Harwell that he and I first became friends. We both enjoyed music as well as physics, and we made much music together—I fear with more enthusiasm than skill, so that the appreciation of our friends had to be tempered with tolerance. We were a young and exuberant society, inspired by doing a fascinating job of national importance. We were led by that remarkable man, Sir John Cockcroft, whose lifelong gift it was, in spite of great responsibilities, to know and to bring the best out of the young people who worked with him. Even then, however, at the age of 26, Hans had had more than his ration of grief. His mother and his sister had been killed by the Nazis, and his father was spared only because of his indomitable courage.

Yet little of this tragedy was visible in his personality. To meet Hans in those days was to get the impression of a carefree youth to whom life and work were a challenge, an adventure, and a joke. He could work with enthusiastic dedication at all hours of the day and night but still retain a vast fund of boisterous energy for recreation, whether it was climbing mountains, making music, enjoying the company of friends, or playing practical jokes. He did everything as a healthy schoolboy would, with a bang. One

9

remembers his inability to shut a door quietly; his vigorous mal-treatment of the piano, where, for him, *crescendo* invariably meant *accelerando,* and *allegro molto* meant *fortissimo*; and his gusts of triumphant laughter.

Hans Kronberger was born on 28 July 1920 at Linz on the shores of the Danube. There he was brought up and achieved distinction at his school. He fled from Austria in 1938, coming to England six months later. He became a student at what is now the University of Newcastle upon Tyne, where he won the Stroud prize in physics, after studies interrupted by internment in Australia. Then, in 1944, he joined Heinz London at the University of Birmingham to work in the Tube Alloys team (as Britain's war-time atomic energy project was code-named), under the leadership of the Oxford physicist the late Sir Francis Simon, and with Simon's colleague Nicholas Kurti. It is to these three men, with whom he worked so closely for six years, that he owed his debt of tutorship. Simon was among the world's most distinguished thermodynamicists, and thermodynamics became for Kronberger a powerful tool. Kurti tells me that it was from Simon too that Hans derived the characteristic outlook of a good physicist, always to peer through the complexity of nature (or of technology) to seek the essential simplicity that lies beneath. He knew that the pencil calculation on the back of an envelope could be more significant than any computer programme, and this was what later made him seem such a formidable interviewer of any luckless candidate who put the trees before the wood.

Kronberger's scientific reputation rests upon the work he started at Birmingham under Simon and continued with Heinz London at Harwell and later on his own at Capenhurst in Cheshire. He was concerned with one of the central problems of atomic energy, the large-scale separation of isotopes, and he worked on almost every aspect of the problem at one time or another. Many of his methods and techniques have now been adopted by laboratories and industries throughout the world. One of his most exciting and difficult ventures during the early days of Harwell was the attempt to separate uranium isotopes with a specially designed ultra-centrifuge. It is to that period that the famous story* of the visit to the Battersea fun fair to ride on the 'spinning wheel' relates: Hans wanted to know what it felt like to be a molecule in a centri-

---

* He related this story to me on the occasion of his appointment as Member for Reactor Development. He and an equally exuberant col-league, wishing to learn more of the (very complex) aerodynamics inside a centrifuge rotor, visited the Rotor at Battersea, where they flipped matches into the bowl to try to gauge the air currents. Soon tiring of this

fuge. The work was prematurely terminated, but it was a source of great satisfaction to him that now, twenty years later, the first gas-centrifuge system is being collaboratively developed by Britain, Holland, and Germany.

Immediately after that project, he made his greatest personal contribution. For he moved in 1951 to Capenhurst, becoming head of the laboratory two years later, a post which he retained after the creation of the Atomic Energy Authority in 1954. There he was concerned with the design, development, and construction of the giant gaseous-diffusion plant for the separation of uranium isotopes on which our nuclear power programme now depends for its fuel materials, and to which he made so many contributions of outstanding merit. It was there too that he came under the influence of two great engineers, Christopher Hinton (now Lord Hinton of Bankside) and Sir Leonard Owen, from whom he learnt the integration of scientific discovery with engineering practice. He freely acknowledged his debt to them; as for their opinion of Kronberger, we have it from Lord Hinton himself that 'the clearness of his composition, the logic of his thought and his absolute reliability made it a joy to work with him'.

That phase in his professional life ended in 1956 as Kronberger began to move up the management ladder, becoming first Chief Physicist of the Industrial Group of the Authority at Risley, then Scientist-in-Chief of the Reactor Group. Finally, in 1969, he became Member of the Authority for Reactor Development. At about the same time he began to play a part in international affairs, becoming a member of the United Nations' Scientific Advisory Committee and of the similar committee advising the International Atomic Energy Agency in Vienna, the latter giving him especial pleasure because it took him back from time to time to his beloved Austria. Shortly before his death he was playing a prominent part in organizing the Fourth Geneva Conference on the Peaceful Uses of Atomic Energy.

His responsibilities covered all the new reactor types under development by the Authority: the advanced gas-cooled reactor at Windscale, the steam generating heavy water reactor at Winfrith, the fast reactor at Dounreay. On one or other of these systems our future national prosperity may well depend. He also took a special interest in nuclear-powered desalination, the process whereby sea-

---

rather slow method of gathering data, Dr. Kronberger's colleague proposed to speed things up by directing a stream of liquid into the bowl. Only by pulling rank, maintained Kronberger, was he able to prevent his colleague from committing an indecent offence. *Editor*.

water is made available for industrial or domestic use, of great importance for desert countries. He had hoped to contribute to stability in the Middle East by means of a large desalination project. Although that failed through lack of capital, his efforts have at least helped to put this country in the forefront of desalination technology.

The nation honoured him with the O.B.E. in 1957 and with the C.B.E. in 1966; the Institution of Mechanical Engineers awarded him the Ludwig Mond prize in 1958, and he was elected a Fellow of the Royal Society in 1965. In 1969, to his immense and still boyish pleasure, he was awarded the Royal Society's Leverhulme Tercentenary medal 'in recognition of his many distinguished contributions to Nuclear Reactor Research and Development and for his outstanding leadership in all branches of this field'. That brief citation stands as a fitting tribute to his personal achievement in technology. It remains to add on behalf of his colleagues only that he brought to the top ranks of the Atomic Energy Authority scientific understanding of a high order, real technological achievement, gaiety and wit, humanity and culture, and above all unbounded enthusiasm. He served his country well.

The authors

Duncan S. Davies ('Creativity and the central laboratory'), aged 49, has been General Manager of Research and Development for Imperial Chemical Industries Limited since March 1969, with responsibility, under the R and D Director, for integration of company research. Previously he had been Deputy Chairman of I.C.I.'s Mond Division for two years. A graduate in chemistry of Trinity College, Oxford, Dr. Davies began work in the research department of I.C.I. Dyestuffs in 1945, and by 1954 was in charge of process research in the division's Grangemouth works. He became Research Director of I.C.I. General Chemicals Division in 1961. The following year he was appointed Director of I.C.I.'s new central research laboratory, the Petrochemical and Polymer Laboratory at Runcorn. Dr. Davies served on the Swann Committee, which reported in 1968 on *The flow into employment of scientists, engineers and technologists*. Dr. Davies is well known as a writer and broadcaster—he is co-author of *Technological economics*—and for his interest in extending the dialogue and cooperation between university and industrial scientists.

D. T. N. Williamson ('The synthesis of ideas'), aged 47, has been Director of Research and Development of Molins since 1961. After studying engineering at the University of Edinburgh, he spent three years in the Development and Applications Laboratories of the Marconi–Osram Valve Company. He joined the research department of Ferranti in 1947, and worked on the first applications of wartime technology to industry, making his name with developments in sound-reproduction equipment. In 1951, after four years with Ferranti, he formed the team that developed the world's first computer-controlled machine tool system; and in 1959 was appointed manager of the Ferranti Machine Tool Control Division. For the past ten years Mr. Williamson has been responsible for the development of cigarette-making machinery and for the application of advanced technology and systems engineering to design and manufacture in light-engineering industries. Elected into the Royal Society in 1968, he is a member of the Engineering Board of the Science Research Council; of the Advisory Committee for Mechanical Engineering; and of the 'Little Neddy' for the mechanical engineering industry.

W. Marshall ('Harwell changes course'), aged 38, is Director of the Atomic Energy Research Establishment, and has also been Director of the Research Group of the U.K. Atomic Energy Authority since April 1969. Except for the years 1957–9, when he was at Berkeley and Harvard Universities, Dr. Marshall has spent his working life at Harwell, which he joined in 1954. In 1960 he became Head of Theoretical Physics, and in 1966—after two years on the Research Group management board—was made Deputy Director. It was in this capacity that he began to implement the changes in Harwell's research policy described in his chapter. Dr. Marshall is a Fellow of the Institute of Physics and holds its Maxwell medal for outstanding work in theoretical physics.

H. W. Pout ('Defence research under pressure'), aged 49, has been Director of the Admiralty Surface Weapons Establishment, Portsdown, since February 1969. Previously he held the post of Assistant Chief Scientific Adviser (Projects) at the Ministry of Defence; a post involving major responsibilities for the advanced technology of all three Services, for the shape of the defence R and D programme, and for efforts to coordinate defence requirements with the interests of private industry. From 1960–5, as Head of Guided Weapons Projects (Naval), he was responsible for the initiation of new guided weapons—principally Seaslug Mark 2, Seadart, and Seawolf—their R and D programmes, and the control of their programmes and finances. Mr. Pout graduated from Imperial College, London, in 1940, joining the Royal Naval Scientific Service to work on direction finding, fire control, and weapon radar. He was awarded the O.B.E. in 1959.

B. T. Price ('Management Science and Government'), aged 50, Chief Scientific Adviser to the Ministry of Transport from 1968–71, is now Director of Planning and Development of the Vickers Group. A graduate in physics of Cambridge University, he worked on naval electronics during the Second World War, shortly afterwards joining the Atomic Energy Research Establishment, Harwell. There his assignments in nuclear physics included work on the Harwell and Windscale reactor designs, cosmic ray research, and measurement of nuclear properties of uranium and plutonium. From 1956 he specialized in the assessment of reactor designs and, in 1959, became Head of the Reactor Assessment

Division, first at Harwell and later at Winfrith. While with the U.K.A.E.A. he also became involved with the international issues of nuclear energy. In 1960 he joined the Ministry of Defence and five years later became Director of the Defence Operational Analysis Establishment, whose main concern is the analysis of options in defence policy in cost-benefit terms.

David Fishlock (Editor), aged 38, has been Science Editor of the *Financial Times* since 1967. Previously he was Technology Editor of *New Scientist*. He has published several books about technology, among them *Man modified* (1969), on man–machine relationships, and *The new materials* (1967).

1

How the atom paid off
By Hans Kronberger, F.R.S.

Πόλεμος πάντων μὲν πατήρ ἐστι.
War is the father of all things.

Heraklitos.

The first internal combustion engine was invented for war: it was a single-stroke engine—the gun. It was half a millenium before the principle of internal combustion was applied for peaceful industrial purposes. The first practical demonstration of the bulk release of the energy stored in the nucleus of uranium atoms was for military purposes, in a gigantic single-stroke 'device'—the atomic bomb. It took only about ten years to develop the first engines in which this newly discovered form of energy could be used for peaceful industrial purposes, and another decade or so to see nuclear power stations being established on a commercial basis all over the world.

The speed of introduction into common use of technical innovation usually exceeds the prediction of the wise old men of science. Perhaps this is because the human mind tends to extrapolate linearly, whereas we are in an exponentially growing phase of human development, where the linear approximation is no longer good enough for predictions extending over a working life.

The Second World War saw the marshalling of vast teams of scientists and engineers on an unprecedented scale into project organizations to develop new technologies in the shortest possible time into war machinery: radar, the atomic bomb, the jet engine, and rockets, for example. When, after the war, Britain decided to establish —to use the delicate nomenclature introduced by politicians—her own nuclear capability, teams of high-calibre scientists and engineers were available from wartime projects, many of whom were already accustomed to working in large, single-minded organizations. From these teams, with a healthy leavening of young recruits from universities, Britain's post-war atomic energy organization was formed, with its first establishment at Harwell. Nuclear capability was generously and wisely interpreted. Yes, there were to be nuclear weapons; but also isotopes for medicine and industry, a large amount of fundamental science, and—the biggest prize of all—the prospect of a new fuel for generating the ever increasing amount of electricity the country would require in the decades to come.

The rapid succession of technical achievements over ten years has blunted our minds and it is difficult now to recall the enormous appeal that the new field of atomic energy had for scientists and technologists, and to the government. We entered the post-war era with a new, untapped source of energy, which promised to remove any long-term fear of fuel shortage. (It is important to remember that in the immediate post-war years there was widespread apprehension of a serious fuel shortage.) There seemed no natural limit to the amount of energy the country could call upon; here was a fuel that could, weight for weight, produce 10 000 times the energy of coal. Nuclear power would not only generate our electricity but also (it was forecast) make the deserts bloom by distilling sea-water, drive ships, trains, and aircraft, and, in the distant future, perhaps power a rocket to take man to the moon. Nuclear fission was no longer a Pandora's box from which came bombs and radioactive poisons, but a cornucopia of technological applications, which attracted the country's most imaginative scientists and engineers. Herein lies the first and most important foundation for the success of the atomic energy project: the high calibre of staff who could be attracted to work in the project, and the government's readiness to provide generous funds.

To those of us who moved into the hangars of the former R.A.F. station at Harwell, those were unforgettable days. No matter that there were at first inadequate supplies of electricity and gas and of stores. Improvisation became a challenge. There was so much to be done, and almost everything was new, important, and useful. It was a situation that would surely arouse the envy of every research manager today.

Research at Harwell

Within the first few years the main activities of Harwell crystallized into an obvious pattern, covering the fields of experimental and theoretical nuclear physics; the metallurgy of uranium and some of the exotic materials chosen for their low neutron absorption; the chemistry of uranium, plutonium, and fission products, and their separation; the separation of uranium isotopes; experimental engineering mainly concerned with methods of extracting heat from a variety of possible fuel shapes; and the field of radiological protection. This was the era of the building of great machines: the accelerators and the piles with which to produce the high-energy particles required for nuclear physics studies, and the neutrons needed for studying the effect of radiation on materials and for the production of radioactive isotopes. The U.K. Atomic Energy Authority, eventually formed to manage Britain's development of nuclear energy, has a strong position in the materials field and in the manufacture of radioactive isotopes and their incorporation into useful compounds that has its roots in the foundations laid at Harwell a quarter of a century ago.

It is difficult for me to recall how Harwell was managed in those stirring early days. Cockcroft was to us young scientists a benign father-figure whose governing hand was felt only lightly. His international reputation made him the focus of world information on atomic energy even before it started to flow freely after the first Geneva 'Atoms for Peace' Conference in 1949; it ensured the influx of high-grade staff and—aided by his political shrewdness—of government funds. Harwell at that time seemed to be impelled by the obvious needs for information; starting rather than stopping work was the problem. As we shall see, it is the latter that tests the skill of scientific management.

Before long, the manufacture of nuclear weapons became a problem not only of providing scientific information, but of producing the materials by a set time. The amount of fissile material in a nuclear weapon may be of the order of ten kilogrammes; but to extract it in concentrated form, several thousand times this amount of natural uranium has to be treated by what are still some of the most difficult chemical-engineering processes known. For the concentration of uranium-235 a gaseous-diffusion plant had to be built: a most complex plant whose technology even today is a closely guarded secret, and which is still one of the greatest engineering achievements of the post-war period. Plutonium in usable quantity did not even exist; this element had to be produced by the transmutation of uranium in large reactors (first the Windscale piles, then the Calder reactors) whose size dwarfed the first experimental piles built at Harwell. Uranium, plutonium, and the fission products had to be separated in a chemical plant based on chemical processes worked out at Harwell on milligramme quantities of plutonium; a plant which was deemed to become inaccessible once operations commenced. And to provide the feed for these plants a factory had to be built to convert uranium ore into fuel elements for the piles and into uranium hexafluoride for the diffusion plant.

The enormous task of building these factories almost simultaneously was taken on by a new group under Mr. Christopher Hinton (now Lord Hinton of Bankside), and centred at Risley in Lancashire. He had a team—small by modern standards—of seasoned engineers who with him had been responsible for building the wartime explosives and filling factories. At first he had practically no scientists in his team, and depended almost entirely on Harwell for the basic information.

The project organization that Hinton set up at Risley to build the basic plants was unique at the time—and it had to perform a unique task. Planning was taken to the extreme, and the 'immutable target date' became almost an obsession. Chief engineers, or directors, were responsible for the various kinds of plants, and under them were project engineers, each in charge of a major unit in the factory to be designed. The project engineer had complete responsibility for all aspects of design and construction.

Project R and D

The project engineers were the pivotal figures in the organization, on whom all design and construction centred; they called on supply and service organizations for support. The pace was breath-taking—multimillion-pound decisions had to be taken on very sparse scientific information, and often changed in the light of new results arriving from Harwell. It quickly became clear to Hinton and his deputy, Leonard Owen, that in addition to the fundamental information from Harwell, a good deal of very specific information was required, closely geared to design. Harwell was not set up to provide this information. Either the research establishment must be changed to a technological development organization, subject to the immediate demands of the Risley project engineers—thereby losing its character as a scientific institution—or a new R and D organization must be created. Hinton chose the latter course. Under Leonard Rotherham he set up the Risley R and D organization, with a technical and theoretical section at Risley, a materials laboratory at Culcheth, and development laboratories at each of the factories under construction. The R and D branch was managed by its director (Rotherham, and later myself); its specific activities were subject to the demands of the project engineers. Development and construction of each plant was managed by one unit, the project committee, in which the engineers and scientists together formulated the development and construction programme and controlled the expenditure. This type of organization proved highly successful—R and D information arrived when required by the project, and alternative solutions were abandoned as soon as they were found unnecessary.

At first, each laboratory had one or two projects, but as the number of projects increased, and specialized skills had to serve many projects, laboratories became characterized by their special skills rather than by projects. Thus the Capenhurst diffusion-plant laboratory became an engineering laboratory (later transferred to Risley), dealing with sodium technology for fast reactors and plant instrumentation and large, experimental test rigs for a number of projects. It then became necessary to superimpose a project organization on the classical laboratory management organization. Thus, the Reactor Fuel Development Laboratory has research managers in charge of ceramics, physical metallurgy, and so on, and chief project officers each responsible for all aspects of the fuel for a particular reactor, irrespective of the laboratory in which the work is done. The research manager reports to his head of laboratories, while the chief project officer's main line of communication is with the chief engineer, or director of the project.

Project control

As the drive to reduce the cost of nuclear power intensified, the sophistication of the development work grew, and more laboratories with specialized technologies became involved in projects. Nearly all the U.K.A.E.A.'s establishments are now involved in some aspect of the fast-breeder reactor project, for instance. More sophisticated methods of control of manpower and expenditure had to be introduced, but basically the philosophy is the old, well-proven one: the needs of the project dictate what should be done, and when. The project management decides what work should be accepted, and charged to the project, and perhaps more important, what work should be stopped. This is done effectively by closing the job account.

A convenient way of illustrating this kind of organization is in the form of a matrix (Fig. 1.1). Each of the laboratories is managed by a 'head of laboratories' (or a division head in the case of major establishments), who has under him research managers in charge of the various sections, such as physical metallurgy, ceramics, and so on, as shown on the matrix diagram. The head of laboratories is responsible for the resources of his laboratory and for the technical content of the work undertaken in it. Each project manager, by contrast, is responsible for setting out a development programme to meet the needs of his project within the total of resources—money and pro-

Laboratory management

Project management	Laboratory 1			Laboratory 2	
	Physical metallurgy	Ceramics	Vibration studies	Heat transfer	Reaction physics
Fast Reactors ⎰ Fuel · · · · ·	⊕		⊕	⊕	⊕
Coolant circuit · · · · · · · ·			⊕	⊕	
· · · · · · ·					
· · · · · · ·					
· · · · · · ·					
Gas Reactors ⎰ Fuel · · · · · ·	⊕	⊕	⊕	⊕	⊕
Coolant circuit · · · · · · ·			⊕	⊕	
· · · · · · · ·					
· · · · · · ·					
· · · · · · ·					

FIG. 1.1. Project management matrix for R and D organization.

fessional manpower—allocated to it. These resources are provided through the usual management channels to the laboratory management, who are therefore responsible for their efficient use. The total resources available to the U.K.A.E.A. are justified by the projects on which they are used, and the project-management side of the matrix makes sure that the deployment to projects is equitable.

This form of management organization, well adapted to the U.K.A.E.A.'s circumstances and well proven in practice, is complemented by a control system that works as follows. First, financial targets are set for each project and agreed generally with the Department of Trade. These targets are incorporated in the project development programmes mentioned above, which aim to meet the technical objectives within the finance available, and which set out detailed targets of expenditure over a period of years with defined technical achievements. These programmes are drawn up by the project management with advice from experts in all the laboratories concerned. Our system presents these programmes in terms of work packages for each laboratory expressed in money and in professional man-years. Subject to the condition that the total requirements of all the projects must be equal to the total resources available, the deployment of money and manpower in each laboratory is authorized for one financial year at a time. As, however, major projects cannot be managed on a one-year basis, expenditure is forecast (though not authorized) on a rolling five-year basis. Second, a record is maintained of the way in which these resources are in fact deployed by projects throughout the U.K.A.E.A.'s laboratories; this provides information that can be compared with the predetermined targets, so that control can be exercised. U.K.A.E.A. projects are reviewed at least once a year, and the actual expenditure and deployment of manpower compared with that planned. The plan for future years is modified if necessary in the course of this review of the project, account being taken of past expenditure and any changed technical requirements, but the total expenditure being kept within the limit agreed with the Department of Trade for the project. Authorization is limited to one year ahead, so as to allow such changes to be accommodated as development proceeds.

It will be seen that the matrix shows both the different kinds of activity within each laboratory, and the different fields of work within each project. The authorization of work by a particular laboratory on a particular project is broken down into a number of individual jobs, with responsibility for each identified with a particular research manager, or man of similar senior level. Each of these jobs has its own manpower and financial expenditure targets, the research manager concerned seeing that the required work is completed, that it is done to the necessary standard, and that it is done within the targets he has been set.

Although this method enables large projects to be carried out swiftly, and within predetermined costs, it does raise the danger of setting too tight a curb on speculative and exploratory work. For this reason, in the U.K.A.E.A., a certain amount of work, although controlled by the scientific management, is not under the jurisdiction of project engineers. This work falls into the categories of 'background and exploratory work' and 'underlying research'. The former category is loosely related to the major projects; the latter is the basic research underlying all applied work carried out in the U.K.A.E.A. Most of the latter is carried out at Harwell.

Discipline

When the project-oriented R and D laboratories of the Risley organization were set up about twenty years ago, fears were expressed that good scientists would not like the disciplines of defined objectives, fixed time-scales, and financial control; that it would be difficult to attract good people to such an organization and to keep them there. Events have proved that this was not so. On the contrary, the feeling of working for a common aim, the knowledge that success would depend on individual contributions, the fact that the tasks to be carried out by individuals or groups were clearly to be seen on the programme breakdown gave an immense feeling of purpose to all the staff.

A large volume of literature exists nowadays on the subject of the management of research and development, with flowsheets of alternative decision-making processes, methods for evaluating the cost-effectiveness of R and D, and discussions of the 'interface problem' between the R and D management and the rest of the management of the concern. Obviously, with the enormously increased complexity and cost of R and D, it is essential to have a clear organization and good methods of cost control; while the extent of national and international competition, backed by large R and D teams, makes it vital to be able to forecast whether the result of the R and D will lead to a competitive product. There are now many techniques—the *software* of R and D management—for dealing with these problems. But for an R and D organization to be effective it is essential to understand also the *liveware*—the staff of the organization; and, most important of all, it is essential to provide the right *input*—the projects and tasks to be tackled.

Many treatises on R and D management refer to an 'R and D organization' as if it were a pre-existing framework, subsequently to be filled with people. The problem is usually the other way around: how to create an organization to fit the people, in particular the key people. Perhaps the most useful advice I ever had as a young scientist was from the late Professor Hanson, Head of the Department of

Metallurgy at Birmingham University. When I was promoted from working at a bench to become leader of a research team, he said: 'From now on you will be judged not so much by your own scientific ability, but by that of the people you can persuade to work with you.' Let me pass on this advice to all future research managers.

The most effective way of attracting good people to one's organization is to offer work on demanding and challenging projects. The majority of scientists prefer to work on urgent projects in need of solutions, rather than to provide solutions in search of applications. In common with all humans, scientists want to feel wanted by and preferably indispensable to their organization, and in general they will feel this way if they have more work to do than they can cope with. In applied science, people tend to give their best when they are under pressure, in spite of grumbles that there is no time to think. Spare time does not necessarily improve the quality of the thinking. Rather, the urgent demands of a project tend to sharpen one's thoughts. The Risley organization has traditionally worked under high pressure, and it has certainly been my experience that people are at their best during particularly difficult periods.

The input problem

The input problem is nowadays by far the most difficult. In the field of civil applied science and technology, governments throughout the world are becoming less inclined to pay for large prestige projects; and industry wants its laboratories not for publicity reasons, but to enable it to compete and survive. The number of projects that could be tackled by the world's technologists is greater than ever, but the number of projects for which governments or industry are prepared to pay is becoming increasingly, and I think rightly, limited. If strict economic criteria are applied, I doubt whether there is now a world shortage of applied scientists and technologists working on research and development, although there may be shortages in certain specialized fields where the growth rate has temporarily outstripped the supply of young specialists.

I always found the input side of R and D management—the introduction of new projects into an R and D organization—by far the most challenging and most rewarding of my activities; far more so than the creation of a smoothly operating R and D structure. Some of these new projects can result from ideas coming up through the organization, a process that should always be encouraged; some come from outside, and form a test of the management's perspicacity and an index of the standing of the laboratory. With a good flow of well-justified projects into a laboratory, the main headache of R and D management, namely, how to stop old projects, ceases to exist. A laboratory manager will rarely admit that his laboratory is doing any work that is not essential, and nowadays he will be able to provide economic analyses to prove his point. The best test of the strength of his arguments is to offer his laboratory a new project *without increase in staff complement.* Knowing that if he refuses it the job might go to a competing laboratory, he will agree, under protest, to put a few people aside to assess the job. If the staff are satisfied that the new job is promising, and likely to grow, proposals will usually follow, showing how, by further rationalization of old work in hand, the new job can be handled by his laboratory.

This reflects the fact that different projects have different degrees of potential economic benefit. The original economic forecasts can be wrong, and frequently are, and even if they are right, some projects are less valuable than others. A laboratory uses the less valuable projects to keep its staff fully stretched until better projects come along.

This displacement technique is a very powerful aid to cost–benefit analysis—and very much older. The only problem then for the R and D manager is to identify the new promising projects, and find financial support for them. I remember that when we were introducing de-salination into the U.K.A.E.A.'s programme the system showed very little manpower that could be made available for the project. Yet within a year a flourishing team had been put together. Similarly, we set up the National Centre of Tribology at the Risley engineering laboratories, which already at that time had a bigger work-load than their complement could carry. Nevertheless, in less than a year, the nucleus of the tribology centre existed and worked. R and D administration systems are usually based on the professional man-year as the unit of effort; but they do not take into account the increased output from a professional man-year if applied to a new and exciting project. This illustrates one of the difficulties of R and D management, that of matching the software and the liveware. The management's job is to interpret the software, which is at best only a guide to action. It is here that management 'flair' enters the picture.

There is perhaps one other human aspect of R and D management that I should mention. Obviously, each R and D organization must have a hierarchy; this presents few problems in an expanding organization, but can produce considerable frustration among the junior staff if the size of the organization has reached a fixed level, or is contracting. The matrix organization, by which responsibility for a project or sub-project can be given across the laboratory hierarchy, occasionally provides the opportunity to give special responsibility to comparatively junior staff, and this can do a good deal to keep morale and output at a high pitch. More often than not, staff whose performance in a routine job has been average start to excel when the spotlight is focused upon them.

I have said a good deal about projects and project organization, with special reference to Risley. This organization has undergone several changes over a period of time, but the project spirit has remained unaltered. It is often said that the heroic age of the U.K.A.E.A.'s giant projects has passed. To some extent this is true. The large plants that form the basis of our nuclear industry are working, a substantial fraction of the nation's electricity is now being provided by nuclear reactors, improved reactor types to supply electricity over the coming decades are well ahead in development. Reactor projects now are fewer, but they are carried out in greater depth. In the early fifties there were perhaps ten reactor types that all appeared equally promising, and exploratory work was carried out on many of them. Only a few have survived as potentially economic power-producers, but today a large amount of work has to be carried out on these few to ensure their reliability and economic competitiveness. The rewards are still very great; in particular the enormous effort on the fast-breeder system is fully justified by potential national benefit. Similar views are held by the major industrial countries, which, like Britain, are devoting a substantial part of their scientific manpower to this reactor system.

Much remains to be done on the established reactor types: the thermodynamic efficiency of gas-cooled reactors can be increased, perhaps eventually by the introduction of gas turbines; the manufacture of fuel can be improved (there is an enormous benefit to be gained from reducing the cost of the uranium 235-enrichment process); and, as I have mentioned, considerable advances are possible in the fast-breeder system, which is only at the beginning of the era of commerical exploitation. Nevertheless, the law of diminishing returns also applies to reactor development. The establishment of a hypothetical new reactor system would cost of the order of £100 million.

The new system would have to be very much better than the sodium-cooled fast reactor to justify its development economically, even on the basis of a world, rather than a national, market. Exploratory studies into new systems will, of course continue, but it may well turn out that the fast-breeder reactor is the last of the major types of fission reactor.

The reduction in the number of large projects was foreseen by the Risley organization many years ago, and the staff complement adjusted accordingly in a controlled run-down that has maintained the pressure of a good work-load on the staff. The skills of managing projects and bringing a wide spectrum of specialized skills to bear have been applied to projects outside the nuclear field. The organization that at first built the plutonium factories for a military programme, and then developed the power reactors and fuel plants for the generation of the nation's electricity, could, given the right opportunity, assist British industry to launch some of the big technological projects that will have to be undertaken to meet world competition.

2

Creativity and the central laboratory
By Duncan S. Davies

For better or worse, the vast majority of able people in affluent western society are now quite highly educated. There are those who say that this education is erosive of the curiosity and enterprise that has been essential in the growth of this society. This view alleges that universities turn many potentially eager fighters into reflective and backward-looking fence-sitters, so concerned with the preservation of the better features of the *status quo* (which for them is comfortable) that they are hungry neither for more wealth nor for further change.

For better or worse also, the key steps in invention and innovation in the past have depended more on the brilliant perception of the social significance of unusual experimental results—penicillin and polythene are examples—than on the systematic, step-by-step reasoning of highly educated men. And for better or worse, wealth generation has depended upon the use of educated procedures of applied logic—engineering, critical-path scheduling, systems analysis, optimization, intelligent planning of human relationships—to develop and exploit the inventions made without the orderly and linear thoughts of orthodox, educated society: although the inventors may, incidentally, have been educated people.

There are those, like Erich Jantsch, who believe that invention will soon become mainly 'normative' and, like manufacture and commerce, will respond to careful and conscious planning. The Instamatic camera contains virtually no new technology, but by simplifying camera mechanics greatly increases the number of good photographs taken and the number of people prepared to attempt good photography. Taking a picture no longer resembles a laboratory experiment: it has deliberately been made more like washing up with a dishwasher. If invention does move rapidly in this direction, then it will become much more compatible with other social—as opposed to artistic—activities, and a basic tension within industry will have been removed. There will then be those who mourn a shrinkage of the world of the artist, and there will be a much weaker case for the industrial central laboratory.

The late Sir Cyril Hinshelwood used to say repeatedly that the big scientific advances—as well as industrial inventions—depended on the big, artistic, imaginative leap to a new hypothetical viewpoint, followed by the logical exploration of its tenability, and the creation of cause-and-effect bridges to current orthodoxy if it made correct predictions and furnished convincing explanations. Yet the consolidation of these advances into bodies of discipline suitable for teaching involved the plodding logic that of itself produced relatively little advance.

Research in the business group

The benefits of good logic and of a high degree of education in the pursuit of defined business objectives are now there for all to see. Indicative capital planning, properly aligned with internal generation of cash and intended (and feasible) borrowing, produces planned and feasible growth in fruitful business areas, and diminished concern with activities and products in which society is losing interest. Selling and manufacture can be planned in double harness, although Europeans cannot accept Galbraith's contention in *The new industrial society* that the large international company derives its markets from its ability to engage in self-fulfilling prophecy.

Western European companies operate within the market mechanism, perhaps unlike some Californian companies, which sell much of their output to massive, organized projects like those of the National Aeronautics and Space Administration. But an atmosphere of unease about the state of the European company's economic climate can be replaced by an atmosphere of confidence in one's ability to forecast the weather far enough ahead to have the ship prepared for most eventualities: if it rains, one is wearing one's oilskins. And this spreads to other fields, such as labour relations; one scans society and its trends, and devises procedures in human interactions that harmonize with general expectation. When our working colleagues are becoming progressively better-educated, we abandon the boss-and-minion ethos that assumes that they are moronic, or likely to be satisfied with the crusts that can be earned by low-grade, mechanical jobs. Machines are introduced, and men are assumed to want to make and repair rather than simply tend the machines. And the men are expected to comment and propose if they think of better methods of attaining the business group's objectives. A job ceases to be 'the fitting of this silencer to this line of vehicles' and becomes 'contributing to the present and future of this business for facilitating communication'. A remark like 'these roads are getting so damned congested that it would be nice to talk to auntie by closed-circuit television rather than buy cars in which to visit her' becomes one that the operative should make and the chairman listen to. Is there a business opportunity here in making a completely new electronics system for the Post Office (or, in the United States, the Bell System) to sell to the public?

Research, at one end of its very broad spectrum, consists of the competent use of logic of this kind, and to this extent we are now spreading the research attitude throughout a properly run business. Departmental boundaries may be necessary, but they are somewhat regrettable. A salesman who contents himself with cursing, rather than seeking to understand the production difficulties that lead to dissatisfied customers, will not devise the best strategy for keeping those customers. And although research must still be done in laboratories and pilot plants, research people must move about, talk to their colleagues, join in strategic discussions, and regard both their cash input and their output of ideas as part of the whole business process— the research cash being an alternative to a straightforward plant extension or an advertising campaign, and the ideas being a product that is preferable to more of the orthodox goods for sale. There are numerous side benefits from this 'research integration', one being that research people move very naturally into other activities such as factory management, planning, or intelligent selling.

Business-group research is thus conducted in an ambience of logic. The research manager's radar antennae scan the business and its environment in a continuous search for opportunities for process improvement, product diversification, changes in raw-material positions that suggest major process research (coal to oil, for example). He looks for new businesses in which his skills promise a better performance in future. He looks for new science that he can unite with his knowledge of social need and opportunity. And in this way he assembles a programme, in consultation with his young men, whose aspirations he seeks to satisfy by the right sort of balance between different kinds of excitement—that of the total innovation on the one hand, that of the new-kindled enthusiasm of the factory manager who is shown how to operate more efficiently on the other. Quick and efficient scale-up is a particularly important area. But the responsible people will want to think of the distant as well as the near future, both in market and in technical terms.

When the sum of the logic of such business research managers provides the bulk of major innovation, artistry will have to be content with music and visual effects for its output. But this time is not yet.

Research outside the immediate business group

The research student who has needed a father-figure (in the shape of his supervisor) finds a substitute, in the business group, in the general logical urgency and command. But there are those who make unusual conjunctions of ideas, which initially do not look very logical, and these are the discoverers and the inventors. We do not know how to recognize or educate them, but we have a suspicion that orthodox educational procedures and business environments sometimes either stifle their originality or deflect their talents into more conventional, logical channels. On the basis of this suspicion, we are prepared to take some action, and to provide a different environment, that will encourage the unusual invention. The more different the invention, of course, the smaller the number of other inventors who will have had the same sort of thought and be filing competitive patents. Logic unites: artistry, initially, often divides. Four crucial business questions are:

(1) What is the optimum amount of social and technical detachment and artistry?
(2) Can it be achieved within a business group at all?
(3) Can it be achieved by a unit supported by a federation of business groups?
(4) Should it be geographically detached?

At one extreme, total social detachment will result in all of the inventions being missed. Send all inventors to work on Mars, and they will not know about the terrestrial significance of a nylon or a penicillin when it is discovered. At another extreme, artistry may be unpractical. We therefore have a need for compromise. There must be recognition of the socially useful result, and there must be some choice of areas of likely technical feasibility, when 'interesting things seem to be happening'. And the inventions, when made, must be developed to the point of demonstrated technical, commercial, and economic feasibility, or no one will build the factory and sell the product.

If young men have, on the whole, more inventive power than older men—and I speak, of course, of averages—then the inventive laboratory must somehow be given the right age distribution; not necessarily one with no older men, but one with the right proportion. If this supposition about age and invention is correct, a laboratory full of fifty-year-olds may still produce some inventions but it will be sub-optimal.

These then are the boundary conditions for the company central laboratory. Different industries, with different histories and different markets and technologies, will devise different solutions. I cannot, in the space available, deal with many cases, and I will therefore particularize now the case I know best—the chemical industry, where chemistry was once almost a sufficient basis, and is now necessary but very far from sufficient. The synthetic-fibres industry, for example, now makes more use of physics and engineering than of chemistry, but would founder if it lost its chemical skills. For us, chemistry is an enabling science, as is mathematics to the whole of technology.

A central laboratory for the chemical industry

Size

A little invention of a really good kind goes a very long way and requires a much larger follow-up. It is therefore feasible for our proposed unit to be relatively small in relation to the innovative research effort in the whole company. As an arbitrary figure, I would say 10–20 per cent of the total. Less than this constitutes a very small voice that may not be heard. More is possible, but then demands that more part be played by the unit in the general run of the business—perhaps with loss of the scope for maverick originality. What is vital is excellent rapport with research and other groups in the relevant business areas.

There is then the question of the effectiveness of the unit size calculated on this basis in relation to the tasks it attempts. Some kinds of research require very extensive support facilities, and these may impose a minimum absolute critical size. Pharmaceutical research involving extensive animal biology and animal screening becomes uneconomic unless many animal programmes are brought together; and work on fibres, plastics, and their intermediates requires a fairly comprehensive assembly of techniques for chemical and physical characterization, and for engineering research and device development. In both of these cases, units with less than 50–100 'prime movers' and spending (in 1971 terms) less than £0·5–1 million annually (including realistic depreciation) are probably too small. At the upper end of the scale, a community with very many more than 100 prime movers is liable to lose the cohesive and purposeful sense of its own power and objectives, and to appear to the young graduate as big and soulless.

Accordingly, the very big company might do well to run more than one central laboratory—each concerned with a different area—if it wishes to employ many more than 100 of these prime movers. Equally, a smaller company, able to afford only a smaller unit, should seek to work in an area calling for less massive support. For example, it is possible to pursue the sort of imaginative work in chemistry that is likely to be useful in yielding more economical processes for existing products—perhaps of rapidly growing importance—with a team of perhaps twenty or fifty graduates. There will have to be a larger element of orthodoxy and definition of targets, and excursions into some fields will need to be discouraged. But there can be plenty of scope for originality.

Staffing

At the sort of size that I am recommending, it is possible to pursue a policy of 'keeping the laboratory young' by exporting the majority of members into the rest of the company before they are regarded (rightly or wrongly) by most managers as too old and too rigid for absorption. At present, this means in most cases that the men must be transferred by the age of 35. This is to declare a belief *not* that it is technically ideal to have most people in the 22–35 age bracket, but that it is impracticable to have them in the 35–45 age bracket if 40 to 45-year-olds from such a unit are regarded elsewhere as unacceptable. In other words, there is no intermediate possible between the policy recommended here, and that of keeping everyone for life. And if such a laboratory is set up over a five-year period, the 'in-for-life' policy inevitably results in later eras in which the average age moves up through the thirties into the forties and fifties.

The 'transfer-before-35' policy implies the acceptance of inexperience (and resultant mistakes) as the price of freshness and minimum frustration. But, in this country, we often do not give young scientists enough responsibility, and it is surprising how much they accept and welcome. Having pursued this procedure for seven years, openly and with full declaration of intent to every entrant, I can claim that it works.

There is an interesting consequential twist. A fair proportion of the 'graduates' of such an institute move out of innovating research altogether when they are transferred. This is because a factory manager or sales manager needing talent will treat his central laboratory as a manpower supplier competitive with his own divisional or business-group research team; he can bargain with both so as to get the best possible man. On the other hand, there is inevitably—and usefully—some degree of competition as well as collaboration between divisional and central research workers, and this can occasionally inhibit transfer.

The important requirement is to arrange and permit the maximum element of choice on the part of the transferees. In some cases, they should move out to develop and help commercialize their own project, so that they transfer their own commitment to the business that will do the scaling-up and selling: the project is no longer held back by being 'not invented here'. In others, they should form contacts and friendships elsewhere, and move, on a basis planned perhaps a year or two ahead, to do jobs they want with new colleagues whom they know they will like. And if a few move back into teaching, this is excellent as a means of helping collaboration with and recruitment in the world of school and higher education—always provided, of course, that the move has not been the result of mutual repulsion!

Geography

The staffing plan has geographical implications: it is best to make the transfers away from the unit as simple and straightforward as possible. This suggests proximity with the bigger future employers. A site in a tree-girt country house may have advantages in some long-term research, but it can sometimes cause protests and difficulty about transfer. But at least one can pick a neighbour who is sited reasonably pleasantly, where housing is not scarce or expensive, and where amenity is reasonable.

Location alongside a big, operating business unit results also in some automatic consciousness of the nature of the business and its constraints: knowledge of market opportunities, of raw-material price changes, and of life in general can be gained across the lunch table or in the staff club. This should not diminish inventiveness in or provoke a conscience-stricken trend toward urgent trouble-shooting (which is the affair of the business group itself). Sometimes, too, proximity may permit the sharing of services and facilities. For example, the engineering load of a central laboratory may be very 'peaky' and best dealt with by a lot of borrowing. Equally, there may be expensive equipment with some spare capacity that neighbouring business groups can use.

The programme

A social institution needs to feel a reasonable amount of esteem, both internal and external. Concentration on nothing but the longest-term objectives can result in long periods with no very tangible achievement, and there may be merit in the inclusion of some work with medium-term objectives and higher probability of success (which, when it comes, is more modest). This need to avoid neurosis is real, but must not be allowed to cause a slide into the short-term work that can always be proved to pay off, if reasonably efficiently done. The choice of the project mix is thus a matter calling for some care and skill. A high incidence of success can, of course, legitimately encourage increased emphasis on the longer-term work.

At the earliest possible moment, however, an incipiently successful project must be shared by collaboration with the business group whose commerce it will be. It is of no use to be for ever dashing into the offices of chief executives waving a test-tube and shouting '*Eureka*'; there must be a plausible market indication, some sensible (if imaginative) process economics, and some sizeable chunks, bags, or drums of the product. Initial reaction will often be sceptical, and it is here that geographical proximity, personal acquaintances, the presence or absence of trust, and a fair measure of political skill count for much.

The ideal outcome is collaboration, culminating in business growth and disengagement of the central laboratory, whose contribution is soon—and healthily—forgotten. But to achieve such an outcome audits that attempt to assess the contribution of the central unit so that it justifies its existence have to be avoided. At best, such audits are inexact: there are many people without whose contribution the project would have failed—how are their relative values to be assessed? At worst, such audits poison the environment with quarrels that seriously inhibit the progress of the next project.

The precise moment at which the central unit can slide out is crucial.

If it has to be postponed, there is less effort available for new invention, if it is attempted too early, the weakly project may have been weaned too soon and die. But it is likely that around half of the staff, at any given moment, may have been assembled for the development of inventions now very likely to succeed. This requires a considerable willingness of people to move from project to project. Fortunately most people like joining in on a success, and this also provides a mechanism for getting failures quietly dropped. It is essential, how- ever, never to drop a project and leave the people concerned in a vacuum while something else is 'thought up'. The good laboratory always has too many good projects competing for too few men.

Organization and motivation

The combination of freedom and order always causes a basic ten- sion, and the organization of a central laboratory needs to be minimal, concerned with policy rather than detail, and as non-hierarchical as possible. There must be confidence in the effectiveness and fairness of the procedures of staff transfer, and in the methods for 'selling successes'. There must be a small group of policy makers, concerned with external relations, concentrating effort on winners, and spotting and seizing on new areas of opportunity. Supporting them there must be a group of area supervisors or coordinators bringing together projects in a rational field of endeavour—say, materials science, or cardiac dysfunction. But these coordinators must not be in their jobs for so long as to become stale.

The greatest and outstanding source of waste in R and D is the project that fails. Failures there will be, and more in proportion to the size of the successes. But it is important that community feeling should be concerned more with the combination of scientific excellence and good project selection than with the minutiae of organization charts or of fussy control of the less expensive inputs. The place must be run safely, and resources should not be wantonly wasted, but there need not be massive concentration on statistics about travelling expenses or test-tubes per man. In a properly run place, individuals can be taught and trusted to be economical and realistic about this sort of thing. Occasionally there will be profligacy and unavoidable waste, but this should not be made the occasion for an *auto-da-fé*.

It is becoming fashionable to seek to quantify research risk. This is acceptable as long as time is not wasted in arguing about index-number differences well within the standard error, or about numbers whose error cannot be estimated. What is far more important is to avoid the technical success that, from the start, was certain to be untranslatable into a business success, and to generate business successes according to the sort of programme that the business needs. For a laboratory of reasonable size, it may be that the indicative planning can rely on the second law of thermodynamics to help in producing the right investment opportunities at the right time. To help in such tasks, the laboratory may need its own small business group—not to enable all others to abdicate from business thought and investigation, but to prevent this from becoming an intolerable burden. Such a team has to work hard to avoid becoming the policemen in an 'us-and-them' situation. And it should be able and willing to buy in good ideas from outside when these can be spotted and made available for purchase.

Finally—dare I say it?—the central laboratory has an indirect purpose. Its existence stimulates business groups, in a spirit of healthy competition, to avoid neglecting longer-term work. This can bring reciprocal benefit: if such effort produces more leads than can be developed, generosity often breaks loose, and some good ideas are then given to the central laboratory. A machine is provided both for collaboration and for the efficient utilization and balancing of the inevitable tensions. Unless the central laboratory is identifiably different from business-group research teams, and pursues extra and ultimately profitable objectives, it has no purpose. Unless it is compatible with them it has no results.

3

The synthesis of ideas
By D. T. N. Williamson, F.R.S.

Professor Sir John Baker, F.R.S., has said that:

'The engineering industry's activity can be divided roughly into four main parts, the design of the product, its manufacture, sale and the management of the overall activity. All are interlocked but design is clearly the most important. If the design is not first class, the product is hardly worth manufacturing since it will be difficult to sell, and so the management effort is wasted.'

Design is central to all engineering activity. In the coming decade, any company that does not realize the truth of this statement will have a very difficult time indeed. Getting the best out of a development department will be a necessary condition for company survival. How then is this to be done?

I believe that one should not attempt to build organizations by the book, but around the people one has, or can acquire. It is people that count—not charts, reports, or statistics—and the whole environment must condition the working arrangements. There is, therefore, no unique, preferred solution, and it is dangerous to think that there might be, and to try to bend an organization to conform with orthodoxy.

The economy of Britain has steadily been losing ground since the Second World War for a variety of reasons, not least because the design concept, quality, and delivery of our engineering products has been inadequate to increase or even maintain our share of growing world markets. If the present trend continues, by the 1980s we shall occupy a position in the European community about level with Portugal. How to get more from our engineering resources, particularly the human ones, is plainly of paramount importance.

In my opinion this is not likely to be done by aping the United States, as many industrialists currently believe. The cards are so stacked that we are certain to lose, because the environmental conditions are totally different, and the effect of the adverse scale factor would be crippling. In fact, I would argue that nothing could benefit the competitiveness of the United States more than for us to copy their activities and methods on a reduced scale.

Engineering manufacture covers a very wide range of capital and consumer goods. The choice of which consumer products to manufacture and which to import is influenced very much by scale and by the need to protect the balance of payments. The problem in a planned economy of whether and what to manufacture is a deep and complex one, but dodging it by *laissez-faire* can lead only to the failure or foreign ownership of whole industries when scale economics come home to roost. World competition in established consumer goods is intense, and, in general, outstanding brilliance in the concept, design, or marketing of a product is necessary to make big inroads into the world market. The alternative is to satisfy the home market, discourage too high a level of imports, and sell the surplus abroad as vigorously as possible. That is what we are trying to do now; but without engineering brilliance even this cannot continue.

Capital goods, on the other hand, are less subject to scale difficulties, and it is possible to compete on level terms. Purchasers of capital goods are usually well aware of their attributes and short-comings, and they buy what they consider to be the best plant for their requirements, substantially irrespective of the country of origin. Cost is less important than performance. In the case of machine tools, for example, we import much at high prices from the United States and Europe, with a severely adverse effect on the balance of payments, simply because the quality or delivery, or both, is better. If it were the other way round, our exports of machine tools would improve significantly. Where it is —in aircraft engines, for example—the picture is very different.

The industrial role of Britain must change during the 1970s. It is vital that new-technology capital products replace those with which we have been familiar for a generation or more, and which are now manufactured throughout the world. It will be possible to spearhead new fields only occasionally, because these usually take too long to become profitable. A more likely role would be to spot and fill the gaps in wider technologies that have been spearheaded by others— in new peripheral devices for computers, for instance. We are basically in a good position to do this, although with the present environment and attitudes it is just not happening. It is a salutary exercise to list the

British companies whose products are better than those of their opposite numbers abroad. After the first half-dozen this becomes hard. It is futile to expect good design to appear in sufficient amount to make a significant difference to the economy without fundamental change in environment and attitudes, both nationally and in individual companies.

Development, invention, and inventors

Development of new products can be either a slow, step-by-step process of improvement, as has been the case with most consumer products and, indeed, much capital equipment as well; or a leap-frogging process of invention and consolidation of a totally new product, or an outstanding improvement, virtually equivalent to an innovation. This second category of invention or innovation is the one of main concern, although step-by-step improvement cannot be neglected. The two approaches are different in character and require different types of people.

Invention, by and large, is a one-man job. The record of outstanding inventions throughout history shows that most were made by individuals not directly connected with a particular organization.[1] While it may appear, nowadays, that invention is performed by a team working together on a project, examination of the patents arising from such teams frequently reveals a common name. The point was emphasized by Sir Alastair Pilkington, leader of the float-glass development team, when he said: 'In the creation of something new, large numbers of people are not an alternative to people of really good quality.'

Typically, the inventor is a craggy, cranky individualist, motivated more by the intellectual excitement of the process than by the possible rewards, who has the will to resist all the people who tell him that it will never work, or that if it did, it would be ahead of its time, and not a commercial proposition anyway. Such men have not been trained to invent. They are naturally gifted, and their early environment has assisted them to develop and employ their gift. This does not mean, however, that creativity cannot be taught—or at least that more of the right type of people cannot be identified and encouraged to think creatively.

Engineers who really make an impact on society are, to some degree, almost entirely of this creative type. Although not necessarily brilliant original inventors, they have the qualities of creativity, enthusiasm, and determination, and are stimulated by intellectual excitement—their primary motivation. When such people are gathered together in the right environment as in the Second World War for the development of radar, the jet engine, and the atomic bomb —tremendous cross-fertilization of ideas occurs, forcing the pace of development. How different is the current situation in Britain— principally because the stimulating environment is no longer there, and the enthusiasm and urgency largely absent. Yet, ironically, we have a situation similar to the attrition of a slow war.

Deficiencies in training

Engineering development has changed considerably in the last twenty years. Instead of the development of individual machines, it has frequently become necessary to develop complete systems, which may encompass several different machines, functioning in concert with much auxiliary equipment, all designed to fulfil a purpose in the most efficient way. A new breed of engineer is required for this *systems approach*. Very few exist at present, and only a handful are being trained.

Engineering education in Britain today teaches a man basic fundamentals—although not always in sufficient depth for modern needs. What it does not teach him is to apply this knowledge to the synthesis of new products, or to develop the type of iconoclastic yet creative outlook required if he is to question old beliefs and replace them with new methods and equipment.

Many university professors assume that, provided a man understands fundamental analytical methods and exercises a little common sense, he has all he will need to be an engineer. This is just not so, and the state of the profession proves it. The majority of teachers of engineering are not creative people, and have little or no understanding of the design process, far less of the complexities of systems engineering and the wide range of knowledge required to be effective. They turn out back-room specialists in their own image. Specialists, necessary of course for research, form too big a proportion of the post-graduate output. This failing is becoming recognized, and steps are being taken by the Science Research Council to improve, for example, post-graduate educational scope and methods. But these, even if successful, will have substantially no effect on industrial research and development for at least ten years—the minimum time it takes for a new graduate to acquire a position of authority and trust from which he can influence new products to anything other than a minor degree. Perhaps I am pessimistic, and change will occur more rapidly, but for the present I would argue that we must accept the fact that creative people will be very thin on the ground.

Where Britain differs

When we examine the industrial scene in the United States, we find that, although there are many large and long-established engineering companies, most of the creative engineering is taking place in small but rapidly growing companies. It is a pattern from which has arisen Route 128 near Boston, and similar mushrooming groups of entrepreneurs in California and elsewhere, usually associated with a university or some military or space research centre. Some grow from nothing to become giants in a few years. Thus the industrial scene is one of constant regeneration and replacement, as biological analogy suggests that it should be. Others, without becoming giants, remain highly successful by giving an expert specialized service. The ingredients these companies have in common are one or two enthusiasts with a bright idea and the determination to exploit it.

Large, older-established companies provide an important service in the manufacture of capital and consumer goods, but only occasionally come up with an outstanding idea (although there are notable exceptions). The best ideas come from the newer companies, and frequently are the sole reason for their existence. If the idea and its execution are sufficiently outstanding, they too will grow accordingly. If not, they will die quickly.

By comparison, the European—and certainly the British—scene is one of stagnation. The environment is simply not right for a small, technically based company to prosper, and comparatively few have managed to win through against the overwhelming odds. The engineering industry is still dominated by companies that have been there for a very long time, many of them famous names, which started on a basis of great invention, but are now well past their best because the initiative and drive of the founder have disappeared. Such companies are being encouraged to amalgamate, tempted by arguments of scale and rationalization. There are merits in these arguments, but it must not be forgotten that the larger a company grows, the more average it must become. Small companies can be selective and therefore get a higher than average performance, simply because the number of people required is not large, and it is possible to find better ones than occur on average in the business community. Although good people are not unwilling to join large firms, their numbers must tend to the average occurrence in the community as the size of the firm increases. The success of the small American company is due to the fact that, while it remains small and vigorous, it can recruit people who are much better than average. As a company grows, statistics dictate that this advantage will be proportionately reduced. Amalgamation simply makes it worse unless attitudes are changed at the same time.

There are three main reasons why the American growth pattern does not occur naturally in Britain. The first is that, at least until recently, financial support to enable innovative companies to grow has not been available without the financier taking control of the company. Once the founders lose control, much of the incentive disappears—and financiers are not renowned for their engineering acumen. Also, the tax structure and the Companies Act do not encourage the growth of small companies—indeed, many would say they discourage it.

The second reason is that in its early days, certainly in mechanical engineering, a small company depends heavily on subcontracting, because finance is not available for comprehensive manufacturing facilities, or these might be considered risky until the product is established. Subcontracting facilities in Britain are far below their American equivalents in quality, cost, and reliability. It is common experience that any small British company that relies heavily on subcontractors is very likely to be bankrupt in six months.

The third reason is that there is, in Britain, no equivalent of the buoyant market for new inventions that is stimulated in the United States by the defence and space programmes, while the European market for new technology is anything but buoyant. Nor, since the American market for such products is mainly controlled by defence, is it possible to export into it, because of the 'buy-American' policy.

For these three reasons, principally, Britain's engineering economy is less fresh and dynamic than America's in new-technology capital equipment. And, as I have argued, this is the one field that could afford products with high added-value and potentially rapid acceptance under conditions much less competitive and scale dominated than for well-established products. Clearly, then, it is very important to change the environment to an encouraging one. It would have the important side effect of creating, naturally, small, highly motivated research groups without having to attempt to organize these artificially from larger groups of more indolent material. The change in national environment, if it happens at all, can be accomplished only by a combination of government encouragement and more enlightened behaviour on the part of finance houses and those organizations that influence the growth, environment, and training and supply of skilled craftsmen. It must be made plain to these bodies that their future well-being depends on it.

The creative environment

Let us turn now from the national environment to that of the industrial research and development laboratory. At one end of the industrial spectrum we have very large companies, with correspondingly large R and D departments, about whose inventiveness and cost-effectiveness experience teaches us to be doubtful. These groups, and their present organization, have given rise to the often repeated statement that it is costing more and more to achieve less and less. At the other end is the small group that knows exactly what it wants to achieve. If it is going to achieve anything at all, it must be by sheer acumen, hard work, and copious use of instinct. In between are the medium-sized established companies where we might find anything from a well-led, effective development department to a few disenchanted draughtsmen in a dusty corner adding chrome-plated strips to a product substantially unchanged for a generation.

Only in the small newly formed group are we likely to find inherently well-directed drive, hopefully capable of circumventing the unfavourable external environment. It must be accepted that conditions in the larger firms are inherently inimical to high-quality R and D, and only strenuous efforts to change these conditions can rescue large-scale R and D from mediocrity. This means a departure from the current fashions in management methods, which British companies are now happily espousing, just when their progenitors in the United States are becoming more and more disenchanted with their lack of results—especially in R and D. As one of the latest American books on the management of innovation contends:

'In both industry and government, a costly and dangerous trend is emerging, a trend toward a kind of management system whose pattern of operation is incompatible with that required for highly creative performance by scientific and engineering people. It is a trend toward tighter budgetary controls and tighter organization of the work. It is brought about by the impact of greater competition and, even more, by faulty information concerning the relative effectiveness of various approaches to cost reduction and improved performance.'[2]

The enemy is size, which brings in its train impersonal management. One defence is to create several autonomous divisions corresponding to product types, each one of which can be self-contained and run like a small independent company. This method has frequently been successful. It gives the management and staff great incentive to succeed, for individual results are not submerged as they are in a large undertaking. Even where a common manufacturing facility is shared, it is worthwhile to keep R and D and sales departments separate, although the result is usually somewhat less satisfactory because of divided loyalties in production, which can become critical. Size is also the enemy of batch production, particularly where there is a wide diversity of products, as effective production control is very difficult to achieve.

The first essential for success in development is to choose methods of organization by which really good creative people can work without feeling constantly frustrated. Remember, as individualists, the very word *organization* will be enough to frighten them off. They thrive best in conditions of near-anarchy, and the less constraint that is applied, without an actual descent to anarchy, the better will be the creativity.

The late Gilles Holst, who directed one of the greatest and most productive laboratories of all time, that of Philips Gloeilampenfabrieken in Eindhoven, practised this philosophy, and his views are worth quoting.[3] Holst's principles, summarized in the form of ten commandements by Dr. H. B. G. Casimir, Philips's Director of Research today, were:

(1) Engage competent scientists, if possible young, but with academic research experience.
(2) Do not pay much attention to the details of their previous experience.
(3) Give them a good deal of freedom and accept their idiosyncrasies.
(4) Let them publish and take part in international scientific activities.
(5) Steer a middle course between individualism and strict regimentation; base authority on real competence; in case of doubt favour anarchy.

(6) Do not divide a laboratory according to different disciplines but create multi-disciplinary teams.

(7) Give the research laboratories independence in choice of subjects, but see to it that leaders and staff are thoroughly aware of their responsibility for the future of the whole company.

(8) Do not try to run the research laboratories on a detailed budget system, and never allow product divisions to have budgetary control over research projects.

(9) Encourage the transfer of competent senior people from research laboratories to development laboratories of product divisions.

(10) In choosing research projects be guided not only by market possibilities, but also by the state of development of academic science.

Dr. Casimir continued:

'It may be said that these principles were established years ago and that times have changed. This is true, and some modifications in organizational structure have been necessary. But at Philips we are convinced that the principles as such remain valid. It may also be claimed that what is right for a large and highly diversified enterprise may not be acceptable for most other industries. Here I cannot speak from first-hand experience. But I have an inkling that many firms—particularly British ones—might do well to consider adopting the principles which proved successful for us.'

Organization must be recognized as a necessary evil, not a goal in itself. A research director's first duty is to make it possible for really original, creative people to work in the laboratories. Where there is over-organization, as is frequently the case in government laboratories, frustration is rife, and it is not possible to attract or retain top-flight people. Much of the prestige of government laboratories still stems from their wartime performance, when the conditions and staffing were totally different, and decision making was swift; and from the post-war nuclear laboratories, which are run by a public corporation, the U.K. Atomic Energy Authority, with facilities and salaries differing considerably from those in the Civil Service, and where the provision of superb accelerator and reactor facilities attracts the best talent.

Sir Vincent de Ferranti, when directing the company that bears his name—one responsible for much more than its share of outstanding firsts in electrical engineering—applied an interesting philosophy. He believed that good inventions leading to good products came about by chance, when the right group of people came together in the right environment; a set of circumstances too unusual and fortuitous to be disturbed. He supported such groups in their original location, even providing them with their own production facilities if needed. At one time, there were four departments in the Ferranti company in different parts of the country developing computers independently. Today this would be shouted down as needless and untidy duplication. Untidy or not, it worked, and the British computer industry today is based largely on its results. The Ferranti Pegasus computer, very successful in its day, started life literally in a group of back rooms in the centre of London. The I.C.L. 1900 range originated in the small laboratory of Ferranti Electric Inc. in Toronto.

The current pursuit of centralization, concentration, committees, methodology, and tidiness so dear to management schools may have its place in large manufacturing and trading organizations. Applied to development, however, it swiftly kills initiative and creativity, and the trend must be put into reverse before irrevocable damage is done. No good development laboratory, from Edison's onwards, was ever tidy, and it would be time to be suspicious if it were. One thing is certain; the more bureaucratic organization and regimentation that is applied to an R and D facility, the more costly to run it will be, and the lower will be the output and quality.

Subdivision of a company has been mentioned as a way of preserving its quality, and where this is not possible I am convinced that subdivision of the development facility is the best way to circumvent the feeling of frustration that 'bigness' automatically produces. All organization should aim at creating family groups or cells, which are as small and self-contained as possible, to fulfil a given purpose. How this can work in manufacturing, and its advantages, I have already discussed elsewhere.[4] The problems in R and D require a different type of structure from that suitable for batch manufacture, but the broad philosophy and aims remain similar. The four aims are:

(1) To achieve the most direct control of all the functions necessary for the completion of the development projects, continuing into the pre-production phase, if the prototype merits it.
(2) To have one man responsible for the project, and to avoid divided responsibility at all costs.
(3) To concentrate the running of the project in one family group located together geographically to give maximum contact and communication.
(4) To avoid the use of service departments as far as possible.

Where these are unavoidable, the services required must be clearly specified and a time agreed for completion. Under no circumstances should design-draughting be provided as a service. The drawing office is an anachronism that cultivates the worst abuses in design.

These aims clearly demand simple vertical organization, with clear-cut responsibilities. In a horizontal organization, with its interfaces and crossing lines of command, frustration is rife, and it is far too easy to evade responsibility. If something goes wrong, it is always extremely difficult to pin down the cause because of buck-passing. American opinion is now very strongly in favour of vertical organization, and it appears to work well, even in big companies. Provided there is a good man responsible for the project, the degree of responsibility should be extended, as far as is practicable, to the creation of a finished product, and in any event must include the pre-production phase.

The interface between design and production

The development of an engineering project is not complete until the product is in production. It is in the early phases of production that most of the problems arise that are expensive to solve, and where the majority of the money is staked. Time-scales are more rigid, and customers expect the performance and delivery promises to be honoured. Yet it is at this critical phase of pre-production, or the commencement of series production, that the project is frequently handed over to less capable people, who may never have seen it before, and who not infrequently tend to behave as if they inhabited a different world from the development engineers who created the product. 'Not-invented-here' attitudes really start to bite at this point.

This dichotomy between development and production is probably the most damaging factor it is possible to have in an engineering company. Some American companies treat a development prototype as something to be redesigned and re-engineered for production by an intermediate department. With American scales of manufacture, this procedure could be justified for an unsophisticated consumer product, if the additional effort and delay were more than balanced by manufacturing-cost savings and increased reliability. But it is a tremendously expensive and wasteful process to do the design and testing twice, and must be considered fundamentally wrong for capital goods. It is also completely against human nature to expect such a system to work. There is bound to be friction, to say the least, between the designers and the redesigners, who are making work for themselves. The designers will develop the attitude: 'Why bother? It will probably be changed anyway!' Here is one of the most cogent criticisms of the currently fashionable cult of value engineering, unless done at the initial design stage—where designer and value engineer are the same person, or at least in the same, close-knit team.

During the Second World War the Glenn L. Martin Company in Baltimore designed aircraft with teams of two on each drawing-board, a designer and a production engineer. Together they considered the design of each section and each component from functional and manufacturing angles. Together they agreed on the best way to make it. This is ideal—but expensive. For most equipment, the same result can be obtained if one production engineer assists about four designers, provided the designers themselves are knowledgeable about production techniques, so that they need to consult the production engineer only for the more difficult problems. The production engineer's main job is then to evaluate each component for cost, production planning, and plant utilization, and to agree its method of manufacture with those responsible for the management of the manufacturing programme. If this is done right through the design stage, and updated with all design modifications, a new manufacturing task can be matched to the resources, and the latter adjusted if necessary by increasing capacity or by subcontracting. There will still be slip-ups, but a fairly accurate picture of production involvement and cost will emerge as the design progresses. Moreover, if this should prove unpalatable, remedial action can be taken from accurate knowledge and in good time.

The management of the design–production interface and its information-transfer system is more in need of development than probably any other aspect of innovation. The development of computer-aided design techniques linking with semi-automatic numerically controlled manufacturing systems shows the way for the future, but the future may never come if we delay tackling the present.

The systems approach

The ideal engineer for advanced product development is one with an understanding of the unity of electromechanical engineering. He must have a creative mind focused like a zoom lens, able to switch from a wide-angle appreciation of the whole wood to a very narrow-angle view of the trees, and even the leaves on the trees, but more particularly the interface between the ground and the trees, because it is here that most of the problems lie buried in the root structure. He must combine specialized analytical techniques with the ability to synthesize in great detail the most effective arrangement of hardware to minimize the control problem.

He must have the charm of Cliff Michelmore, the drive of a tycoon, and a fairly detailed knowledge of the range of engineering disciplines involved in his hardware. Otherwise the hardware specialists will quietly confuse him. He must have a deep sense of urgency and responsibility for the whole project, and the judgement to know when to insist on getting his own way and when to give way.

Such an engineer is likely to be familiar with structures, transmissions, mechanisms, oil hydraulics, servomechanisms, control engineering, and computers, and systems that combine them all. Such men are very rare, for they are the product, not of specialized training, but of experience. The project leader must have a good understanding of these disciplines, even if it is unlikely that many others in his team will. The best that can be hoped for is that the individual members of a newly formed team will have specialized knowledge, probably in greater depth than the team leader, and that the combined coverage will be adequate. If they are thrown together with good communication, and provided with opportunity for frequent discussion, each man's knowledge will rub off on the other members, until they all have a multi-disciplinary approach. Deliberate measures should be taken to encourage this interaction.

As a supplement to a wide technical capability, a good systems engineer will be versed in the art of handling people, and getting the best out of them, and in the art of project management. Mostly this is a matter of aptitude and common sense, but there are techniques worth acquiring. A considerable amount has been written on this subject, much of it of American origin, and unfortunately most of it mediocre. But an interesting report by P. R. Whitfield of a visit to the United States to discuss creativity in engineering is well worth reading for its ideas and references, as a guide to the best American thinking about education for innovation.[5]

The product team

The number of people in a product team should not exceed about ten. Difficulty of communication is one reason, but this is also about the maximum that can be led properly by one man. If a greater effort is necessary, it is preferable to use teams in parallel, and to give one of the leaders over-all responsibility. Provided that leaders are carefully chosen and imbued with common purpose, this can work well. But any attempt by one leader to score off the others needs to be suppressed quickly.

A typical product team for electromechanical design might consist of, above all, a project leader—responsible for everything connected with the project, including the quality of its specifications and other documentation and costing. He may require an assistant or assistants to look after these things and leave him as free as possible to devote his time to ensuring that the level of creativity and the quality of engineering are adequate. In a project-design team, the specification may already have been issued by a systems-design team, who will take responsibility for the design of the complete system and the correctness of product specifications, so that they will perform adequately when combined in the system. This latter situation gives the product designer less leeway for modifying the specification, should difficulties arise, as changes may produce a chain reaction with the other elements in the system. The other members of his team will be a senior mechanical designer and mechanical designers; a senior electrical designer and electrical designers; and a production engineer.

Mechanical engineering has hitherto been a very slow-changing art, and the type of manufacturing facilities in a given company tends to set the pattern for component design. Electronics, on the other hand, is changing at a tremendous pace, and it is prudent to treat electronics design and manufacture as a central group, so that the techniques used may be standardized as the latest that it is desirable to use in the company. If this is not done, a very wide range of techniques is liable to arise as each engineer becomes acquainted with the latest semiconductor 'wonder'. Incorporated haphazardly in different products, these devices can give rise to an impossible situation in manufacturing and maintenance.

It is necessary, of course, to upgrade these techniques continually—but in a controlled manner. Under present conditions, a good way is to maintain a central facility, and allocate engineers from it to a given product team. Their prime responsibility is then to the team leader for the correct functioning of the electronic content of the design, but they use central facilities for the design of circuits and their mechanical layout, making use of the full repertoire of techniques maintained by the company. Their secondary responsibility is to the chief electronics engineer, who in turn is responsible for the quality and technological content of the electronic design. Where a range of products of a similar nature is established, and separate production facilities are available, the need for this standardization of techniques is less pressing, but any company would be wise not to let them run wild. The senior electrical designer has therefore to collaborate with the team leader to meet the specification of the electrical side of the complete design, and has to guide the remainder of his team, and be responsible for the complete design and manufacturing specification of this equipment to standards determined by the chief electronics engineer.

As I have emphasized above, close working proximity between the mechanical and electrical engineers is of paramount importance, not only to reduce misunderstandings, but in order that the two disciplines shall cross-fertilize.

The production engineer has a very great responsibility, and he must be carefully chosen for knowledge, level-headedness, firmness, and charm. His duties change as the project matures, and may be listed as follows:

Early formative stage. Provision of information that will guide the project leader in selecting basic design strategy, as this may be affected by production resources.

Preliminary layout stage. Specific problems on construction; cost estimates and manufacturing information for alternative methods.

Detailing stage. Advice and guidance to detailers on methods of production and cost; keeping records of finally selected methods; guidance on design for chosen method of manufacture; preparation of parts lists, and issue and scheduling through prototype manufacturing shop; ensuring that suitable production methods are used at this stage.

Prototype assembly stage. Observation of difficulties and possible improvements; keeping records of information for subsequent production, including total cost and time estimates, etc.; alternative recommended production methods for follow-on production; general rationalization of the design for manufacture.

Fully engineered, factory-tested pre-production stage. Issue of drawings, parts lists, computer-aided design tapes etc., each with recommended production methods; conferring with pre-production engineers to ensure that the implications for manufacture are fully understood.

The production engineer of the design team has to be an effective bridge between design and manufacturing, and has to earn the respect of both functions. He will usually be supported by manufacturing services such as cost estimation and tool design where appropriate.

Service departments

It will frequently be impractical to have such specialists as materials engineers, plastics-design and tooling engineers, fluid-power engineers, and computer personnel in sufficient numbers to complement each team directly. Moreover, it is essential for the development of these disciplines to have groups greater than the size that could normally be sustained within each product group. These groups will normally be set up as service departments, from which people can be attached to a design group for as long as is necessary, or where, more usually, advice can be sought when required.

The relationship between the design groups and the service departments is important. The service to be supplied should be defined and agreed as far as possible, even if this definition has to be changed several times throughout the project. There should be checkpoints at which the service can be seen to have been supplied as arranged or not, if disagreements and evasion of responsibility are to be avoided. It quite frequently happens that a task, thought to be simple, allocated to a service department and partially forgotten, turns out to be critical and paralyses the whole project.

Systems group

Where the product involves systems engineering—as will happen increasingly—the product-design teams work to specifications produced by the systems group. Detailed discussion of the organization of a systems group is beyond the scope of this chapter. Suffice it to say that the problem is again one of communication, and although the formal communication must be by very clearly written specifications, close day-to-day communication is very important, so that the nuances that it is impossible to convey in a specification, and which tend to change all the time, can be understood by all concerned. There is no substitute for close geographical proximity and frequent informal discussions between the principals concerned. Formal conferences do not bring to light many of the stumbling-blocks that beset systems engineering.

Again, personality counts nowhere more than in a systems group. It is essential to display a helpful attitude, drawing out difficulties and worries, and making sure that a common interpretation of the task prevails, and that there are no misunderstandings.

Conclusion

Getting the best out of a development department is essentially a human-relations problem. I find it difficult to convey on paper, especially in the confines of a chapter, the fine nuances that relations with people necessarily involve, particularly with touchy types like good engineers! And the better they are, the more difficult they are. There is no substitute for trust and mutual respect built up by personal example. No fashionable management clichés will fill the gap if trust is absent. Leadership, inspiration, creativity: these are emotive words. Either you have these qualities or you don't, and no paper-pushing organization can be a substitute for them.

The trick is to formulate a working arrangement around the people you have, which will not discourage but will actively encourage them to give of their best. Follow the broad principles of vertical responsibility and build small, tightly knit groups, which at least should ensure good communication and control. And remember that, if it were easy, there would have been no need to write this book.

References

1. JEWKES, J., SAWERS, D. and STILLERMAN, R. *The sources of invention.* 2nd edn, Macmillan (1969).
2. ALLISON, D. (ed.) *The R and D game*, p. 169. M.I.T. press (1969).
3. *Sci. J.* **5**, no. 7 (1969).
4. *Proc. Inst. mech. Engrs* **182**, part 1 (1967–8).
5. Institution of Mechanical Engineers, 4 November 1968 (unpublished).

4

Harwell changes course
By W. Marshall

The Atomic Energy Research Establishment at Harwell is a large multi-disciplinary laboratory employing 5500 people, of whom about 1200 are qualified scientists and engineers. Up to 1967, all were engaged on science and technology for nuclear energy. By 1970, a substantial part of the laboratory had been redeployed on new work in support of industrial objectives other than nuclear power. At the time of writing (June 1970) 30 per cent of the staff and 25 per cent of the budget have transferred to the new industrial objectives listed in Table 4.1. This was a major change to make in so short a period, and in this chapter I shall discuss the difficulties we had to overcome in achieving this change.

The twenty-four years since Harwell was founded by its far-sighted first director, Sir John Cockcroft, have seen many changes. During the first few years our main task was to establish the scientific background for Britain's plutonium-producing reactors and the chemical separation plants for fissile material. During this period the first British radio-isotopes were produced and marketed, and we helped hospitals, industry, and many others to exploit this new tool. (Later, the Radio-chemical Centre at Amersham took over this new industry, building up to a turnover exceeding £3 million, over 50 per cent of which is exported.)

During the 1950s the first steps were taken at Harwell towards the development of economic nuclear power reactors. Among the systems studied then were the fast reactor and the high-temperature gas-cooled reactor; systems of international importance today. Harwell grew rapidly in size and to limit this a new establishment was founded at Winfrith, to which reactor physics and engineering studies were transferred over the years 1958–60. Similarly, the U.K. Atomic Energy Authority's plasma physics and controlled nuclear fusion

TABLE 4.1.

Harwell's industrial portfolio 1970

Processes

Desalination (NN)
Heat transfer and fluid flow (NN)
Reverse osmosis—water renovation (NN)
Reverse osmosis—liquid food products (NN)
Bio-medical technology (NN)

Food sterilization and preservation (N)
Extraction of uranium from sea-water (N)
Radiation chemistry (N)
Physical chemistry (N)

Environmental

Atmospheric pollution (NN)
Marine technology (M.A.T.S.U.) (NN)

Hydrological tracers and coastal sedimentation studies (N)

Materials

Isotope separation (N)
Heavy-element studies (N)
Ion implantation (N)
Mechanical and physical properties of solids (N)
Materials Technology Bureau (N)
Ceramics centre (NN)
N.D.T. centre (NN)

High-temperature fuel cells (NN)
High-temperature chemical technology (NN)
Carbon fibres (NN)
Analytical R and D unit (NN)
Physico-chemical measurements unit (NN)

Tribology centre (NN)
Activation analysis (N)

Computers

Computer optimization (NN)

Computer software (NN)

Instruments

Tracers and radiation (N)
Small power sources, e.g. RIPPLE (N)

R and D in aid of uranium supplies (N)
Electronics research (N)

N: nuclear.   NN: non-nuclear.

programme, also centred at Harwell, was transferred to the new Culham Laboratory from 1960 onwards. Harwell's work in high-energy nuclear physics, which included the design of the 7-GeV proton accelerator, Nimrod, was transferred to the Rutherford Laboratory in 1961. From these major transformations Harwell emerged as primarily a materials research and development laboratory.

In Chapter 1, Dr. Kronberger describes how the original goal, set in the 1950s, of competitive nuclear power has been achieved, and how the Authority pioneered in Britain the assessment of programmes on the basis of cost-effectiveness. The turning-point came in 1965, when assessments showed that, for Britain, nuclear power was fully competitive with other methods of electricity generation. It then became clear that, although development of the third generation of British power reactors would require a lot of work, the scale of effort would be diminished. This led us to examine Harwell's future role, and to conclude that, although Harwell's original mission was not at an end, if the laboratory were to continue with a healthy programme, it would need a major new additional mission to justify it. Nor was it too difficult to decide what this additional mission should be.

It had been argued at times in the past that in some way Harwell should play a role in higher education. But on examination that did not seem a plausible mission for a government laboratory set up and staffed exclusively to do research. Furthermore, there had recently been a major expansion in higher education and there seemed no place nationally for a new initiative of this kind from Harwell. On the other hand, it was recognized that a major national need was the encouragement of technological advance and innovation in British industry, to help improve the economic well-being of the country. In this general area we believed we had the scientific background, facilities, and experience to make a contribution. We therefore concluded that our future mission must be as a general scientific research laboratory assisting British industry.

But was our conclusion valid? We thought it was plain that Britain needed more research and development oriented to industrial problems, but we were not sure initially what part Harwell could or should play. We knew we could undertake scientific research on a wide range of problems and that we could use our resources to develop ideas rapidly, and we saw this was essential to meet international competition. Furthermore—and perhaps most important—we knew that the laboratory could rapidly change its orientation and objectives. But the simple idea that national growth and innovation were linked closely with R and D had been largely discredited (as Pout shows in Chapter 5); it was fairly well established that R and D could be almost worthless unless done as an integral part of an operation linking them closely to design, production, and market. This point was subsequently emphasized in the report of the Central Advisory Council for Science and Technology on technological innovation in Britain, July 1968.[1]

Against an industrial mission

The question we faced was therefore quite clear: for our new programmes, could Harwell work so closely with industry that our research was strongly and properly motivated, and so be really effective?

We naturally had ideas ourselves and received others from government circles and industry. We identified a few arguments in favour of an industrial mission for Harwell—all advanced by us—and we also identified a large number of arguments against the general idea, mostly drawn to our attention very forcibly by other people. I shall review the arguments for and against, then go on to say which ones turned out to be real and which proved fictitious.

All these arguments were in our minds at the same time, and all were unresolved: therefore in order to capture the spirit of the managerial problems involved in changing the course of the laboratory, I shall begin by listing them without resolution. It is worth stressing, however, that the mere fact of identifying eighteen arguments and questions to be answered, and writing them down, is itself a partial rationalization of the position we found ourselves in. At the time, of course, we did not identify all the arguments clearly—in fact, we had no real evidence to suggest that the number of adverse arguments was even finite. To be specific, we saw the following problems.

(1) It was argued that we were too expensive. Harwell is a well-equipped laboratory, and industry could not afford the same sophisticated level of equipment; it was argued therefore that industry could not afford to use Harwell.

(2) There would be too much staff inertia. The change we planned was of such a magnitude that it would need the whole-hearted cooperation of the staff, and since this meant that many of them would have to abandon lines in which they had specialized for many years, they would resist it. Moreover, they would not be keen on the new programmes because they did not have the same intrinsic scientific interest and would, in any case, involve collaboration with industrialists and industrial laboratories far from Harwell. Our best people would be unwilling to stay.

(3) We would overlap with the Research Associations. There existed in Britain over forty Research Associations, each with

excellent connections with its own industry. If we also did industrial research, how could we avoid competing with the R.A.s; and if we tried to avoid competition, how could we possibly find industrial business?

(4) Isotopes offered an obvious place to start a programme of industrial exploitation. The section already devoted to the exploitation of isotopes and radiation, detached from the main body of Harwell in a separate laboratory at Wantage near by, had for many years worked very closely with British industry. This effort had played an important role in promoting the use of isotopes and radiation in British industry. We were proud of this work, both because the sale of isotopes had started at Harwell before transferring to Amersham and because subsequent work at Wantage had developed new applications for isotopes and radiation. Unfortunately, we simply could not see how to justify, even to ourselves, increased work on isotopes and radiation along these same lines.

(5) It was not at all clear how far (under the new Science and Technology Act of 1965) we could legally go in expending our R and D outside the terms of the 1954 Atomic Energy Authority Act.

(6) What worthwhile ideas did we have? They seemed pitifully few at the time.

(7) Even if we were to succeed in setting up an industrial research programme on this scale, it would consist of a large number of small projects, each with its own objectives. The result would inevitably be an enormous hotchpotch of opportunist effort, which, abetted by the need for strict commercial security, would soon destroy the coherence of Harwell's research.

(8) If we were going to do industrial research it was self-evident that we should start by consulting industry about the wisdom of this. This was not done in any systematic way, but we took every opportunity to discuss the possibility of Harwell entering the industrial research area. The checks we made were random, but the response was entirely unambiguous. Industry simply did not want us, and most people sought strongly to discourage us.

(9) We were not market-oriented, so our research could not be well motivated.

(10) We could see for ourselves that in the past there had been a general argument that more scientific research eventually filtered through to make a better technological innovation and therefore a better balance of payments situation. But we could also see, so

tenuous was the connection, that the argument carried little weight. In close analogy to this argument it followed that anything done at Harwell was inevitably remote from the production line and from points of decision, and therefore would be ineffective.

(11) We had little commercial experience. Nor was it plausible to think that our scientists could gain suitable commercial experience while in the Harwell environment.

(12) We had no commercial organization and, quite clearly, if we were to do industrial research of a commercially valuable kind, we should need an organization to negotiate terms and to protect our industrial property. (In fact, we already had a small commercial office but on a scale that was quite inadequate.)

(13) The idea was not credible financially. The scale of industrial research that we were contemplating was far too large; we were thinking of something like a third of Harwell—an expenditure of £4–5 million a year—which was very much larger than any contract research laboratory in Britain, and indeed in Europe. We estimated that we would need to be associated with innovation in industries, or sections of industries, commanding a turnover of £500 million a year. It was not plausible to think that we could go from a small-scale industrial effort to such a large-scale effort in a short time.

In addition to these thirteen specific problems, there were four rather general problems we had to face during the period from 1967 to 1970.

(14) Britain was going through a state of economic crisis (which resulted shortly afterwards in the devaluation measures of 1967).

(15) The nuclear power industry was reorganized and, in consequence, there was a natural uncertainty about the future of the Authority itself and about Harwell in particular.

(16) There was a widespread mood of self-examination and criticism of the country's scientific and technical performance. Two particular aspects of this critical thinking were a violent swing of opinion against science for science's sake and simultaneously a strong feeling that in Britain too much scientific research was done in government-funded laboratories compared to that done in industrial laboratories.

(17) The early days when Cockcroft started the atomic energy project at Harwell were incredibly exciting. There was a general feeling in the country at large, and indeed among our own staff, that those

'good old days' were the best we should ever see. To a modest extent, therefore, we had grown into the habit of looking backwards at earlier achievements instead of forwards at new possibilities. This was bad for our morale.

Finally, if we ignored all these problems, one still remained.

(18) How should we begin? What problems should we tackle first?

For an industrial mission

To set against all these points of difficulty, we could see for ourselves only a few arguments in our favour. First, we had an undoubted ability to do research—and to do research to strict time-scales (see Chapter 1). From our nuclear experience, we knew what the industrial environment was like, and we had the ability to put together teams of scientists, technologists, and engineers in any desired combination. We were not therefore concerned about our technical ability to do research that was defined.

Second, we could see that, in principle, we ought to be able to achieve a strong synergetic effect whereby an atomic energy research programme assisted the industrial programme, and vice versa.

Third, we could see that, in well-defined and specific cases, industrial firms might find it more straightforward to contract research to us rather than recruit their own research staff. We saw that this contract research would be particularly convenient when the research required know-how and disciplines of a kind that the company did not normally possess; for example, a chemical company might ask us to study a problem that was primarily of physics content.

Fourth, as a laboratory we had a strong incentive to make a success of a new programme. As management we wanted to do everything possible to assist the national interest. It was attractive to think that we could take a useful part in meeting the economic problems of Britain. We saw that the scientists would be motivated to this end equally strongly. We saw that if we could succeed in the new programme the success would have a useful by-product, namely, we should survive.

Not all the arguments and problems set out above have yet been resolved, but on most of them we have fairly clear opinions. Some problems turned out to be fallacious, others, non-problems. I shall deal with these first.

Fallacies and non-problems

The argument that our research is too expensive to interest industry (Problem 1) is simply fallacious. We have now had the opportunity to offer our research services to industry, and we find that their cost is acceptable. It is true that a scientist at Harwell costs marginally more than a scientist in industry, and that is because he is using more support effort and more sophisticated equipment, but on a value-for-money basis our industrial collaborators have not found costs inhibiting.

Problem 2, that there would be too much inertia for the scientists to be interested in new opportunities, also turned out to be fallacious. A large number welcomed the opportunity to do something exciting and new. Industrial research, it turns out, is as great a challenge intellectually as atomic energy research.

Problem 3, that our industrial research would be bound to overlap with the Research Associations, turned out to be a non-problem. We have discovered that there is so much to do, and the opportunities are so wide, that there is no need or temptation for us to compete with the Research Associations, who are already doing an excellent job, each in its defined field. Harwell's abilities are different, and the initiatives we have taken have therefore been of a different kind. It is of course true that, because of their widespread industrial involvement, we have come into contact with them many times. As a result, we have set up a number of joint research efforts so that each may contribute its expertise to the solution of a problem. For some of these joint projects it seems common sense for Harwell to take the major responsibility for direction, but in many cases we act as the junior partner. In this way we are able to contribute specialist Harwell know-how to the project while leaving the broader issues to the Research Association, which is more familiar with the problems of its particular industry than we are.

Real problems—but soluble

Another group of problems turned out to be real but of such a character that we thought our way through them fairly rapidly.

Problem 4, that it seemed impracticable to build on the nuclear work we were already doing in association with industry, took some time to solve. Gradually we came to realize that this was because we had always looked upon this work with something of a missionary zeal. We had interpreted it as our national duty to keep industry in general informed about the potential uses and advantages of isotopes and radiation, as techniques that could be applied in a wide variety of cases. I am quite sure that this missionary approach was well justified in the early days of the project. To illustrate this, we recently asked the Programmes Analysis Unit to examine in depth and in retrospect the work of one group, the industrial physics group. The P.A.U. conclusion was that the work 'has led to substantial financial benefits of the order of some millions of pounds to the U.K. economy'. But missionary work of this kind brings diminishing returns as general knowledge of isotopes and radiation becomes widespread, and, therefore, for as long as we retained the existing objectives of the programme, we could see no reasonable alternative to a gradual decline in the scale of our existing research programme. We therefore rethought the objectives of the work and identified a number of cases where projects could be re-focused in a sharper way, in collaboration with individual firms, and directed at fairly short-term commercial objectives. Once we had begun to identify a few projects of this kind, all our thinking began to fall in place and the whole programme gradually transformed itself into a set of sharply defined projects, each with its own mission. In summary, Problem 4 was real but it had been resolved by changing from missionary to mission-oriented work.

Problem 5, the legal position, was a difficult one. It was not legal for us under the Atomic Energy Authority Act to undertake industrial research, and, although the Science and Technology Act of 1965 contained an enabling power for the Authority to undertake work outside the original terms of the 1964 Act, each addition needed the personal approval of the Minister responsible. Each new idea was therefore exposed to a careful process of scrutiny, first by Harwell, then by the Authority, and finally by the Ministry itself, to make quite sure that the general idea was in the national interest, and that the work we proposed did not overlap or conflict with the work of any other government organization.

Inevitably, this process of seeking a 'requirement' from the Minister to apply our science to new objectives was time consuming, and in the early years of our new programme absorbed a good deal. Naturally, it was frustrating for the scientists to have identified their new ideas and new projects, and then have to set them aside until the Minister had given us the legal authority to pursue them. But the whole process was very important, and certainly had the effect that we put a great deal of care and attention to thinking out the general programme we wished to follow. After about two years we had received authority for a number of projects, and these, broadly speaking, cover our main areas of expertise. This legal problem, then, was a real one, but one which is now eased.

Problem 6 ('What projects could we possibly propose?') worried us for a relatively short time. Once we had made the decision in principle to pursue industrial research, it encouraged the individual scientist to come forward with proposals. Quite soon the question became instead: 'Which shall we choose of the large number of projects coming forward for consideration?' This selection process itself involved thought, of course. But naturally we found it much more satisfying to be making a selection from several good ideas rather than wondering what ideas we had at all. So many promising ideas came forward that the industrial programme grew very rapidly in the course of a two-year period. Indeed we would now see no difficulty, in principle, in making the scale of our work twice as large. Because we had a large number of ideas to choose from, we were able to select those that fitted in best with our previous experience in atomic energy, and so build up a portfolio of projects, which, while diverse in objectives, had strong relations one to another, and to the atomic energy programme in the scientific sense.

This we feel has had an important effect in minimizing the effect of Problem 7, the multiplicity of technical objectives. It is true that the Harwell industrial programme consists of a large number of relatively small projects or sub-projects. Each has a defined objective and, of course, that objective differs widely from one case to another. But, because all these programmes have been grafted on to the atomic energy programme in a natural way, there is an underlying scientific coherence, and this has been important in enabling the laboratory to function in a coherent way; it enables projects to keep in touch one with another, and encourages the scientific discussion within the laboratory that is quite essential for our future.

Industry's attitude

Problem 8, that industry simply did not want to work with us, was naturally an extremely important one, and a difficult problem to overcome initially: there was no short-cut solution. We could only change the attitude of industry by demonstrating that we could be helpful and effective. We decided that the responsibility for setting up a dialogue and communication between industrial firms and ourselves was clearly ours.

Our first step was to make contact with as many companies as possible, to identify their problems and their possible interest. We encouraged our scientists to visit industrial companies and try to identify the real industrial problems and to define those problems on which it might be appropriate for Harwell to work. We set about making better contact with industry on a quite massive scale. At one time perhaps a hundred of our staff spent a sizeable fraction of their time visiting factories and industrial laboratories. Indeed, we joked that we were abandoning science and becoming salesmen instead.

This conscious act of policy did, however, have very beneficial effects. First, industry learnt at first hand about the capabilities of Harwell. More importantly, it made us think of the industrial problems in a realistic way, which helped us enormously in developing our own ideas. Gradually this intensive effort of establishing communication with industry brought forth results, and as we established more and more industrial links quite naturally the attitude of the industrial companies to working with Harwell changed.

Fortunately, it turns out that we do not need to have such a massive sales effort on a permanent basis, although from those early days we have learnt how important it is to pay attention to communications. Projects must be defined in such a way that both the research scientist and the production engineer know exactly what is involved, although they tend, through their background and training, to use different vocabularies.

The real and difficult problems

Four problems, in the event, caused the most difficulty. These were Problem 9, the fact that there was an intrinsic difficulty in orienting research to the market-place, particularly if the research is not in the parent company itself; Problem 10, that we were remote from the production line and therefore remote from points of decision; Problem 11, that we had no really deep experience of industrial research and commercial thinking; and Problem 12, that we had no commercial organization to negotiate contracts with industry and to guide us in our general approach to problems. It is convenient to discuss these four simultaneously.

We were extremely conscious that we were weak in these four areas and initially we did consider the possibility of setting up a strong central commercial organization, using experienced people recruited from outside Harwell to direct our work. But the more we looked at that idea, the less attractive it seemed. We had some doubts whether we could attract people with the commercial background necessary. We had even greater doubts about outside people grasping rapidly enough the breadth of Harwell's scientific abilities. But, most of all, we were worried by the fact that a central commercial organization would merely act as an interface between the scientists and industry, so that the scientist would think about science in a rather academic way, and would not really turn his mind to the questions of commercial exploitation. He would not then really feel involved in the industrial work and he would thus have no real motivation to make it successful; in short, he would not be market-oriented.

On the other hand, the alternative to a strong central commercial organization was not easy to contemplate. It was simply that the leader for each individual project would develop a commercial understanding, obtaining experience rapidly enough to guide the industrial exploitation and negotiations with industry, in addition to directing the research in his project. In a sense, this alternative would involve us in turning a sizeable number of scientists into businessmen. Prospects of success did not seem too high.

Nevertheless, this was what we attempted. We decided we had no alternative, and, as each project or sub-project was launched, we set in charge a project officer with responsibility both for its scientific content and the commercial goal. Initially, the response was mixed, and we had some difficulties in drawing the boundary between the responsibilities of the project officers and those that we thought were problems for our small central commercial office. But after an initial period of uncertainty, most project officers responded to the new challenge with great enthusiasm. Because we were all inexperienced, and because we were all scientists, we fell very naturally into the position where each project officer would expose his commercial thinking to his colleagues for their criticism and comments. In this way, we learnt very rapidly one from another. We learnt very rapidly that, for each project, it was important to get a very clear idea of the market we were aiming for and to establish a good understanding and feeling of mutual confidence with our industrial colleagues.

'Principle of maximum unfairness'

From the outset we adopted one general principle when thinking of the exploitation of ideas generated inside Harwell. We argued that, since the market is all-important, and since all the research we did involved a high risk, it was essential that everything should be oriented towards a successful market exploitation. This meant that our research had to be motivated by a market we had defined in discussions with our industrial colleagues. Furthermore, in order to compensate for the risk of the research, it was important to work with one company exclusively on any given idea. The logic of this seemed irresistible. The British market is small compared with the world market, and in any case most new ideas have to start off with a small initial market. It was, therefore, most important that this market should not be divided. A single company, we felt, should be helped to a dominating position, strong enough to resist the competition that was bound to develop from overseas. This policy of choosing a single industrial partner for each idea, to the total exclusion of all others, as the normal method of exploitation, was relatively new for a government-funded body. It was rapidly dubbed the policy of 'maximum unfairness'. This policy was not a Harwell invention—certainly it had been discussed previously at some length within the Ministry of Technology—but I think we can claim to be one of the first government-funded organizations to put it into effect on a substantial scale.

In all our discussions with British industry we have found an almost unanimous acceptance of this policy. This policy is important not only because it gives the chosen company the maximum possible advantage in the market-place, but also because it has a large number of secondary advantages. For each idea, once we had committed ourselves to one company exclusively for exploitation, that company and Harwell had an identical, unambiguous motivation, namely to make a commercial success of the idea. It meant that the company was prepared to talk quite frankly to Harwell about its marketing plans and difficulties. It meant also that Harwell's scientists were very thoroughly committed to the project.

The policy of maximum unfairness is not always easy to carry out, because it involves us in selecting a particular company—to the exclusion of all others—to be our industrial partner. There is, of course, no guarantee that we will make the choice of partner correctly—no magic formula by which we can do it. Nevertheless, it must be done. After a few occasions where we relied too much on logic and our own attempts at commercial analysis, we recognized that the most important factor of all in deciding whether an industrial collaboration would work or not was the attitude of our collaborator's management. If the chairman or managing director was enthusiastic, the project would go well. If not, the project would go badly.

To sum up, then, we learnt very rapidly that the market is all-important; this leads immediately to the principle of maximum unfairness. Furthermore, very thorough communication has to be established between Harwell and our chosen industrial partner; this requires an enthusiastic interest from the top management of the firm and a strong sense of involvement from our own scientists. Given these conditions, all other problems are easily solved. For example, when our own scientists and those of our industrial partner are working as a single team to meet a specific market objective, then questions such as: 'Shall the work be done at Harwell or in the industrial laboratory?' become quite irrelevant. The work is simply progressed in the best possible way. Thus often industrial scientists work at Harwell in the research stage but Harwell scientists work in the factory during the later development stages of setting up a pilot plant. In this way, we cease to be remote from the production line (Problem 10) and we are heavily compensated for our lack of deep experience of industrial research (Problem 11). Furthermore, since we have decided to place the major responsibilities for exploitation, as well as science, on the project scientists, our need for a commercial organization (Problem 12) is brought down to a reasonable scale. Perversely, perhaps, it seems that our initial lack of experience and commercial organization was in the long run an advantage to us, because it obliged us to learn these lessons so carefully.

General problems

I include in the list of difficulties four rather general problems, 14, 15, 16 and 17. All four have certainly made our task difficult. Because Britain endured an economic crisis leading to devaluation, our budget and, more important, our manpower, has been severely restrained as an economy measure (Problem 14). Obviously, it is not easy to set up new programmes, such as our industrial programme, and simultaneously cut back hard on the total research programme; yet that is what we have had to do. The next problem, concerning the reorganization of the nuclear industry and the consequent uncertainty of the

Authority's future, fortunately has not yet had a direct effect on Harwell's research programme. The third general problem I mentioned was the swing in public opinion against long-term science in general, and against science in government-funded laboratories in particular. It obviously affected the general climate in which we work, but in general we believe it is right that there should be more emphasis on technology as compared to science, and an increase of research in industry—though not simply as an alternative to government-funded research.

The change of emphasis in Harwell's programme has brought a fair share of public interest, and that has been very good for the morale of the Harwell scientists. We have also been encouraged by favourable references to the Harwell programme in Parliament. For these reasons, problems of morale, caused by nostalgia for the excitement of the 'good old days', are now, I hope, largely eliminated (Problem 17). But the most important factor here was the close personal interest taken by a number of very prominent industrialists, who have taken the trouble to visit Harwell over the last two years to see exactly what we were doing. We are very grateful to them for the interest they have shown and for the morale boost that each visit gave.

Two problems remain on my list of eighteen. Problem 13 was concerned with the financial credibility of the new operations and Problem 18 was 'How should we start?' We never did solve the latter; it just happened! I shall therefore concentrate on Problem 13. We have taken the view that, although our primary objective must be to work to the national interest, yet we should also attempt to optimize the commercial return to Harwell. Thus, while the ultimate factor in whether or not projects should be undertaken is the national benefit that we see flowing from it, we consider it extremely important to obtain for Harwell a financial return. So we pay a good deal of attention to our financial balance sheet.

It is still very early days indeed to make any careful assessment of our industrial programme as a whole. It is notoriously difficult to sell research; the returns on it are necessarily uncertain and necessarily delayed for many years. Now, and for some years to come, it will be possible to have only a broad indication of the way the programme is working out. Nevertheless, the start we have made seems to be encouraging. In the last three years, not only has the industrial programme grown rapidly in size (see Table 4.1), but the percentage cash return to Harwell has also grown rapidly. Three years ago we had received in direct cash payments for our work only a few per cent of the relevant expenditure. In 1970, we expect the relevant expenditure to be larger (£4 million) and to receive about 20 per cent of this in direct cash returns. In addition to this direct cash income we also expect a future royalty income from successful research projects. This source of income is difficult to forecast, but we have estimated it as carefully and cautiously as we can, and concluded that the value of the royalties on work we have done so far, when discounted to the present day, amounts to about £1 million.

As this expenditure covers projects for which we expect no financial returns—such as research on atmospheric pollution—and also the cost of a large amount of advice and small-scale consultation for industry, the present rate of return seems to be a good beginning. We expect this return to increase as our interaction with industry grows.

Reference
1. *Report of the Central Advisory Council for Science and Technology on technological innovation in Britain.* H.M.S.O. (1968).

5

Defence research under pressure
*By H. W. Pout**

The manager of research and development, like any other manager, must first ensure that he has his facts and aims correct. To set a correct course, he must know his present position, the intended objectives, and the cross-currents and obstructions to be expected *en route*. Unfortunately there is today a vast smoke-screen obscuring not only the far and middle distance but even the immediate surroundings. This smoke-screen is compounded of ignorance of the available facts, special pleading by scientists who should know better, and the general managerial inefficiency of scientists and research engineers. It will not be fruitful to discuss defence research and its relations with the economy generally until I have dispersed some of this smoke-screen.

R and D, whether good or bad, appropriate to needs or inappropriate, will always absorb wealth. Unfortunately there is no such certainty that it will generate wealth, and herein lies the central problem of the R and D manager. The converse of this statement is also true—wealth can be generated rapidly without any significant expenditure on native R and D. The United States became the wealthiest country in the world towards the end of the nineteenth century, some fifty years before she devoted a significant proportion of her resources to R and D. In fact, two things led to massive American spending on R and D: her immense wealth made it easy to do so, and the military threat, first from Germany and later from the Soviet Union, provided the incentive. Considerations of economic growth had no part in the reasoning, and even today play little part despite the *a posteriori* rationalizations of special pleaders. Tables 5.1 and 5.2 compiled by O.E.C.D. in 1967 from data for 1963–4, illustrate these and other relevant points.[1]

* While the author gratefully acknowledges the permission of the Ministry of Defence (Navy) to publish this paper, the opinions expressed are his own and do not necessarily reflect official policy.

TABLE 5.1

National R and D objectives 1963–4

Country	Proportion of R and D expenditure (%)		
	Nuclear, space, defence aims	Economic ends	Welfare and miscellaneous ends
United States	63	28	9
Britain	40	52	8
Germany	17	62	21
France	45	41	14
Japan	<5*	73	25 (approx.)

* O.E.C.D. estimate.

The heavy concentration of American R and D expenditure on space and defence is striking; for Britain and France it was also considerable.

TABLE 5.2

R and D resources in 1963–4

Country	Gross national expenditure on R and D (G.E.R.D.)			Qualified scientists, engineers, and technicians employed on R and D
	Total G.E.R.D. (U.S. $ million)	Per head of population (U.S. $ million)	% of G.N.P.	
United States	21 075	110·5	3·7	696 500
Britain	2160	39·8	2·6	159 540
Germany	1436	24·6	1·6	105 010
France	1299	27·1	1·9	85 430
Japan	892	9·3	1·5	187 080

Note: The use of official exchange rates tends to exaggerate the difference between the United States and other countries in the first two columns of figures.

The heaviest spenders on R and D are the United States and Britain; the fastest growers are Germany and Japan. It may be relevant—although no relationship has yet been proved—that Germany and Japan, with less than two-thirds of Britain's rate of spending on R and

D, devote a considerably higher proportion of that spending to economic and welfare ends.

The strong negative correlation between spending on R and D and the rate of growth of national wealth is shown in Table 5.3.[2]

TABLE 5.3

Correlation between R and D and growth

Country	R and D as % of G.N.P. 1950–9	Average compound rate of growth of output per man 1955–64 (%)	G.N.P. per head 1964 ($)
United States	1·7	2·0	3200
Britain	1·5	2·6	1700
U.S.S.R.	1·6	4·2	(1200)
Germany	0·5	4·4	1800
France	0.6	4·8	1700
Japan	0·5	8·8	600

Note: The second column of figures relates to a period five years later than the first column, to allow time for the R and D to bear fruit.

We cannot, however, explain the fact that the G.N.P.s of Germany, France, and Japan have been growing at several times the rate of those of the United States and Britain on the assumption that expenditure on R and D *reduces* the growth rate of the G.N.P., without stretching credulity to breaking-point. What then is the explanation ?

There is perhaps a clue in some interesting data assembled by Professor Bruce Williams from O.E.C.D. sources,[2] on which Table 5.4. is based. International comparisons of this kind are subject to considerable error; nevertheless, it appears that although Britain, Japan, Germany, and France have about the same proportion of Q.S.E.s in the employed population, smaller proportions of these are employed on R and D in France, Germany, and Japan, the fast-growing countries. Statistics on the employment of the remainder are not easy to find, but it would be a reasonable guess that manufacture and marketing predominate. Column 4 suggests that there is a somewhat closer correlation between economic growth and the proportion of Q.S.E.s *not* employed in R and D! Table 5.3 provides some support for the view that higher growth rates are easier to achieve with lower levels of wealth per head (provided the 'take-off' point has been

TABLE 5.4

Employment of qualified scientists and engineers
(Q.S.E.) in 1962

Country	Q.S.E. as % of American total	Q.S.E. as % of employed population	% of Q.S.E. in R and D	% of Q.S.E. not in R and D	Q.S.E. per 10 000 of employed population	
					In R and D	Not in R and D
United States	100	1·7	33	67	56	112
U.S.S.R.	(120)	(1·8)	(20)	(80)	(36)	(144)
Japan	40	1·3	(15)	(85)	(20)	(113)
Britain	20	1·0	25	75	25	75
Germany	19	0·9	15	85	14	77
France	14	0·9	17	83	15	75

Figures in parentheses are estimates.

reached), and that wealthier countries spend more on R and D than poorer countries (making due allowance for the effect of strong political motivations). But none of the correlations is very good, and we must conclude from Tables 5.3 and 5.4 that there are probably several factors that affect the rate of economic growth, native R and D being one of the least significant. Perhaps managerial motivation and efficiency are two of the missing and more significant factors. This affords, I believe, an interesting and important hypothesis.

The role of R and D

Before the reader leaps to any unwarranted conclusions from this somewhat destructive analysis, let me make a further point: while there is every reason for doubting that native R and D is a crucial factor in economic growth, there can be no doubt about its significance where it is desired to carry technology to the limits of achievement. New products, ahead of contemporary competition from friends or enemies, demand native R and D, often in large amounts; in no area is this more apparent than in the fields of space and aircraft. Defence provides many examples. Such projects will normally fail the simple tests of the accountant; discounted cash flow studies can be relied upon to halt them in their tracks; city financiers will keep their hand in their pockets when invited to assist; only the most optimistic market researchers provide any encouragement. Usually in such circumstances the government is expected to pay, but even here resources are not unlimited and criteria of selection are necessary. Clearly the defence research manager is faced with these problems in a particularly acute form.

In civil life, not many decisions take this most extreme form. There is usually a spectrum of possibilities between minor improvement and major advance, allowing management to choose any criteria for commercial success that it may favour. In defence, however, the pressures are usually for the major advances; the price for failing to achieve these advances can often be presented in a stark form by military staffs.

Defence R and D and economic growth

I have already demonstrated that native R and D is probably not a very significant factor in the economic growth of the country. As Table 5.5 shows, defence R and D is a falling percentage of the total British expenditure on R and D, and even less likely to be a significant factor in national growth.

TABLE 5.5

British defence and total R and D expenditure

	1961–2		1964–5		1966–7	
	£ million	% of total	£ million	% of total	£ million	% of total
Defence	246	37	255	33	266	26
Total	658	100	771	100	883	100

Against this background, it is unlikely that the simple, direct transfer of money or resources from defence R and D to the civil sector can have more than a trivial effect, particularly since about three-quarters of Britain's defence R and D spending is with industry already. Clearly something more subtle is indicated.

Three basic needs

But first let us clear a little more of the smoke-screen. I would emphasize that, just as the budget of the Department of Health is

6

voted for health purposes, the defence budget is voted for the purposes of defence, and this must take precedence. Nevertheless, it would be short-sighted if the Department of Defence, in attempting to increase the nation's ability to survive by military means, wilfully reduced its chance of economic survival, and in fact it does not set out to do so. My opening paragraphs, however, indicate only too clearly how difficult it is to decide on the correct criteria, even for civil R and D, where rapid economic growth is sought. Defence is not even an economic activity, to which accounting conventions and normal financial judgements can be applied—it approximates most closely to life insurance, a field where one hopes at all times to avoid the return on the investment. The defence R and D manager is therefore faced with attempting to associate non-economic factors with commercial criteria. This is virtually unexplored territory, analogous to life insurance with endowment and profits!

He begins with several handicaps. He knows that his young staff will have been brainwashed from an early age by teachers and professors into believing that 'basic' research is the height of attainment for a good brain; that 'applied' research is for lesser thinkers, and engineering for the near-failures. Britain has an outstanding record in basic science, but its very strength is damaging to the nation. The young scientist or engineer will have learned no economics—although he will usually hold the beliefs I exposed as fallacies at the beginning of this chapter. He will know even less about management, beyond, perhaps, holding the view that it is a rather disreputable and parasitic activity—for a scientist, a clear admission of failure. A little later in his career he will complain bitterly (and rather illogically) that scientists nearly always seem to be managed by non-scientists. Until this curious atmosphere has changed, much of the education of the modern worker in R and D will have to be given after he leaves his university. He will have to learn the elements of national economics—where money comes from, what it represents, and what the owners of the commodity expect from those who are permitted to spend it. He will have to learn how to manage people, how to plan the use of men and money, how to test progress, and—even if only crudely—how to measure success. He will also have to learn that narrow specialists are especially privileged people and can be afforded in small numbers only. The great majority of scientists must demonstrate a degree of versatility and a width of knowledge appropriate to the demands of a time when success comes most often as a result of cross-fertilization between disciplines, and often only at considerable cost in highly qualified effort and other resources. The days are past when important scientific laws could be discovered with the aid of materials to be found in any well-filled dustbin. Even in the nineteenth century material wealth was created largely by practical engineers with no theoretical knowledge—theory and the associated intellectual wealth came later.

Thus education is the first task of the defence R and D manager. Without it he will be attempting to sculpture stone with wood-working tools.

The second task is to build a suitable organization. A large defence R and D establishment, if it is to run smoothly, must include three clearly defined elements—planning, research, and projects—each with its own terms of reference and criteria of success. *Planning* is the process by which a large number of disparate pieces of work, each with its own programmes and requirements for resources, are brought together to form an integrated whole, matched to the available total resources and linked by the common factors of defence policy. It should be a continuous, dynamic process embracing a ten-year span and must include career planning for the staff. The word *Research*, in this context, I use in a particular way. It covers those activities that must precede the formulation of a military 'target' or requirement, and includes assessment of options, experimental work to clear up the more important scientific and technical uncertainties, and basic work on such things as the components of systems. Research must be distinguished from *projects* because, although there must be objectives with associated resources for most of the research programme, costs will generally be smaller and the pressure on time must be less severe. Projects will be based on formal requirements and will be closely controlled in time, resources, and performance. In short, the atmosphere in which projects are pursued must be 'taut' by comparison with that of the research department.

The third requirement of the defence R and D manager is a sense of purpose that can be conveyed to his organization. Even the best organization will fail without primary and secondary objectives that can command the respect of all, and inspire some. If all organizations had clear and acceptable objectives there would be much less talk of the need to tailor organizations to the people in them. The Army has never found it necessary to tailor itself closely to the 'psychology' of its recruits.

Given these three basic needs, what can the manager hope to do? The primary aim of defence R and D must continue to be the improvement of the capabilities of the armed forces, the purpose for which the defence budget is voted by Parliament. Nevertheless, Britain's defence budget is tightly controlled and has been falling in real terms for several years—a process not yet complete; it is essential therefore to seek good value for money. Much more than in the past, the likely performance, costs, and programme of military equipment are closely scrutinized, and the possibilities of collaborating with other countries, and of foreign purchases, are taken into account. This process of assessment, while it may delay the start of full development of projects, helps to avoid costly and damaging cancellations; it should provide industry with a better picture of future intentions and lead to more saleable articles; and on the whole, it tends to eliminate at an early stage the most extreme forms of weapons, or at least leads to a more cautious approach to such weapons. Considerations of value for money, leading to the elimination of costly projects, the search for collaborators, and the cautious approach are reflected in the fate of the TSR 2 aircraft, the naval fixed-wing aircraft carrier, the Anglo-French variable geometry aircraft, military hovercraft, and others.

Such a technological assessment should be of some direct benefit to the economy. Although the very advanced weapons have provided, it is true, a great challenge to the research worker, and led to rapid progress in such fields as aircraft and radar, the general unbalancing effect on the economy of rapid and expensive advances in some branches of science and engineering, bought at the cost of neglect of others, is bad. So-called 'fall-out' from the advanced field into others is small and bought at great cost. Britain is suffering from the attraction of most of our best mechanical engineers into the aircraft and aero-engine industry. Rapid developments in electronics have not been accompanied by corresponding advances in the mechanical design of electronic equipment; for example, the mechanical design of vehicles and radar-aerial mounts has fallen behind. What is more, the physical sciences, which lend themselves to exact theory and controlled experiments, have outstripped the social sciences, public administration, and management generally, which do not. The deleterious effects on the modern world of these distortions are now becoming very clear.

As there is at least the circumstantial evidence advanced earlier in this chapter to suggest that management quality and manufacturing skill may be more important factors in ensuring economic growth than technological fall-out from R and D, it is well worth considering how spending on defence R and D might be directed towards improving industrial management, without disturbing the main aim. We can best achieve this by giving industry as far as possible managerial responsibility for defence projects, and, through appropriate forms of contract, offering the greatest possible incentive to efficient management and the adoption of good practices.

The contractor should be involved deeply in the project study that precedes formal development. This study, moreover, should be designed to cover not merely technical aspects and costs of the coming development but market-research and sales aspects, production-cost forecasts, whole-life costs with their impact on design for reliability and easy maintenance, and the time-scale. This stage must be followed by the preparation of a good specification for the development contract. The more complete this specification, the closer to a fixed-price contract it should be possible to get. If this can be combined with prime contractorship, the contractor has the greatest possible incentive to be efficient and to devise an effective management system. Such contracts can often combine R and D with a production order, thereby encouraging control of production costs and efficient manufacture too. If the specification can embrace whole-life costs, a further incentive is introduced to design for good reliability and economical maintenance. If a degree of cost sharing between government and contractor can be introduced, linked with foreign sales prospects, this encourages attention to the requirements of foreign customers; in any case, market research should be included in the project study. Where foreign collaboration appears worthwhile as a means of sharing R and D costs and reducing production costs with longer runs, the specification should be designed to encourage this. In this way defence can also make a contribution to the broader political aims of the nation.

The defence establishments

The complementary roles of the defence R and D establishment in such a collaboration must not be overlooked, for they are crucial to the success of these more enlightened procedures.

First, there is the assessment of military problems and the interpretation of military requirements in technical terms. Only if scientists and engineers are in close and constant contact with military policy, strategy and tactics, and intelligence, and with the officers concerned in these activities, can they provide the support required by the military and the guidance required by industry. Such men, far from being a barrier between industry and the military staffs, are an extension of those staffs. They are extremely knowledgeable, and independent of particular industrial pressure groups or firms, with a wide appreciation of what is going on in other countries, and capable of making an unbiased and honest choice between options.

Second, there is the research programme, which enables the establishments to generate the new knowledge required against the background of military needs and assessments, and to prepare for the next generation of weapons and equipments. Although it is carried out partly in-house and partly extramurally, the close knowledge of military problems possessed by the defence establishments enables them to plan and supervise this programme effectively. The establishments also take part in the numerous information-exchange projects that exist within such bodies at N.A.T.O. Out of this work develop the military staff targets, which lead in turn to feasibility studies, staff requirements, and project studies. Industry should be brought in at all stages, but, until sufficient progress has been made to enable a precise specification to be written, the project development phase cannot begin, and the fixed-price or incentive contracts cannot be placed. To perform these various roles, and carry out the evaluation and acceptance that must follow development, requires high quality teams. It is a primary duty of the R and D manager to develop and maintain this quality in his establishment.

Such establishment activity must also be carried out efficiently, and the organization I discussed earlier is essential to its success. Good people must be selected and developed, and important, attractive work must be available to hold their interest. A poor quality establishment would be worse than useless. An organization is not a machine; neither is it just a complex of interacting human beings. It is something with a purpose or task, and the organization chart, the information flow, and the human complex should be controlled and motivated by that task. But at the same time the establishment must be enlightened in its dealings with industry, be ready to give industry responsibility wherever this is feasible and likely to benefit the companies concerned, and to disseminate knowledge as freely as possible. Both industry and the establishments need to devote more attention to the questions of why a project is required, to choosing cost-effective solutions, to whole-life costs rather than initial costs alone, to taking a wide view of both problems and solutions, and to good management. For this they should seek to encourage schools and universities in producing a new kind of scientist and engineer—for which I have already provided the specification.

In sum, education provides our human material, science adds to our knowledge, R and D adds to our technological capabilities; but efficient manufacture and marketing add to our wealth. Each one of these requires efficient management.

References

1. *The overall level and structure of R and D efforts in O.E.C.D. member countries.* Organization for Economic Development and Cooperation (1967).
2. WILLIAMS, B. R., *Technology, investment and growth.* Chapman and Hall (1967).

6

Management science and government
By B. T. Price

Complexity of government is part of the cost we pay for the benefits of science. Rapidly increasing populations, pollution, the squandering of natural resources, a world so lavishly supplied with communications that it has no time to reflect before a decision is due, a power of self-annihilation, the ceaseless creation of mutually competitive new technologies: these are all consequences of the revolution in physical and medical science of the last two hundred years.

Science unfortunately progresses in an untidy and haphazard way. A new discovery carries with it no guarantee that the problems it creates will also in their turn become more tractable. The great decrease in infant mortality since 1800 implies nothing about increased agricultural productivity. Nor will the successful completion of Concorde necessarily show us how to eliminate the bang. Moreover, the judgements needed to deal with the consequential administrative problems are not always those that scientists are accustomed to make. For all of these reasons, science, having itself created the problems, has—except in wartime—largely stood aside from the business of grappling with them.

But in the past few years there has been a change, a distinct swing towards a direct involvement of the scientists themselves in the problems of public administration. A deliberate attempt to see how far the traditional approach of science—observation, hypothesis, deduction, and test—can usefully be brought to bear in such a radically different and novel field. In this chapter I shall suggest some of the influences that have led to this change of attitude, and some of the ways in which the techniques of science are now beginning to be employed at the national level in Britain.

The change had its beginnings in the Second World War when—as part of the major managerial upheaval brought about by the conflict— a number of scientists of outstanding quality were pressed into service as advisers to the armed forces. Their intellectual ability was such that they were naturally consulted on major issues of war policy, issues which at times lay far beyond those that would normally be regarded as within the scientists' bailiwick. They devised new intellectual tools to assist in this process of management, and greatly developed the methods of operational research—which an earlier generation of scientists in the 1914–18 war had also used but which, in the inter-war years, had been largely ignored.

Perhaps because of this further development, it was easier in 1945 for the wartime methods of scientific management to take root in the post-war world. The process was assisted by a number of other favourable circumstances. New science-based industries, such as atomic energy and electronics, were already being developed, and young scientists inevitably found themselves being drawn into management. Secondly, there were for the first time more scientists than could be absorbed by the traditional occupations of teaching and research, so that the pressures of the employment market played a part. Thirdly, the established and powerful methods of operational research, and the dramatic increase in computing power (which started in the 1940s and is still continuing) led to an entirely new ability to marshal facts, to test relationships and interactions and to explore the likely consequences of a range of policy options—a capacity that has obvious relevance to the problems of senior management.

But the growth to maturity of a whole generation of scientists has itself exercised a very profound influence. By the 1960s the wartime scientists had become leaders in their own right. Blackett was Adviser to the Ministry of Technology and President of the Royal Society. Zuckerman was Chief Scientific Adviser, first at the Ministry of Defence and later to the whole government. Below them were scores of men still in their forties, who had been closely associated with national policies for the best part of twenty years. It was entirely natural that this generation should wish to apply itself to the major problems of the day; inevitable that once it had done so it would be struck by the fascination and intellectual challenge of public administration; and hardly surprising that it should go on to discover that here was a field with a capacity for exploiting the benefits of careful research that matched anything the normal scientific or academic worlds had to offer.

At this point it would be as well to clear up a small matter of professional nomenclature. Most of the readers of this book are, no doubt, practising scientists, or are seriously considering a scientific career—using the word scientist in its normal sense of physicist, chemist, biologist, and so on. But the subject matter of this chapter lies a little apart from that of the rest of the book, in a somewhat ill-defined area bounded by economics, the physical sciences, mathematics, operational research, and in some cases sociology. The approach is, and has to be, multi-disciplinary; and even though the majority of the practitioners are traditional scientists—this being a straightforward matter of market availability—the contribution from the other 'boundary' professions is of the greatest importance. We are short of a generally accepted terminology to cover this whole field of work. Operational research, econometrics, systems analysis, and social science all play a part; but I shall use the deliberately general term 'management science', and trust that those who are economists will be forgiving if, for brevity, I use the term scientist without further qualification. After all, no less a person than the President of the Royal Society has described operational research as 'a branch of economics'.

With such an inter-disciplinary field to be covered, it is not surprising that no one profession can be regarded as the natural leader; and in practice chance and the accidents of history have had a good deal to do with the present distribution of tasks. In Britain the wartime effort that laid the foundations of operational research as we know it today was basically a creation of experimental scientists. It was therefore a natural development when, in 1964–5, the then Secretaries of State for Defence—faced with increasingly difficult problems of resource allocation—decided to encourage a more analytical approach to policy-making, and to build a new operational analysis organization round the teams of physical scientists who had continued to work alongside the armed forces since the end of the war. But in the Ministry of Transport events followed a different course. In this case, perhaps because the problems facing the department were more those of investment appraisal than any consequences of radically new technology, the drive for better analytical capability owed a great deal to the Ministry's economists. They set up a new group to carry out mathematical modelling, along lines very similar in approach and technique to that done by the operational research groups of the Ministry of Defence.

This then, is the background. I shall now describe some of the approaches to problem-solving that I believe have proved useful, indicating the limits beyond which they are unlikely to be able to offer much assistance, and how the work meshes in with the rest of the administrative machinery.

Military management science

Military operational research, nowadays a highly theoretical subject, began as an observational science. The very high level of activity in wartime meant that there were always events to be observed, statistics to be interpreted, policy lessons to be derived. Admirably short links existed between the operational research teams working in the field and the highest levels of command, so that reactions could be quick and definite.

The work covered every aspect of operations. Although the statistics available were only marginally adequate for his purpose, Blackett was able to argue, and the Navy came to accept, that naval doctrine on convoy protection would be substantially improved by adoption of the large-convoy policy. The Royal Air Force used operational research much as a large business nowadays uses work study, to the great benefit of all its operations.

The scientists of Coastal Command, for instance, noticed that on the average more U-boats were sighted on one side of an attacking aircraft than on the other. They pointed out that this was apparently contrary to the laws of symmetry; traced the anomaly to differences in work-load between the pilot and co-pilot; and finally suggested a simple method of effecting a useful improvement. They also analysed in detail the process of actually making an attack on a U-boat; developed tactics suitable for the somewhat inadequate depth-charges then available; demonstrated that a change of aircraft camouflage would substantially improve the chances of coming up to a submarine before it had dived; and furthermore developed statistical methods of calculating U-boat densities with some precision, which in turn could be used to estimate where the balance of advantage lay at any given time in the continually changing struggle between aircraft and submarine.

A most significant application of operational research to the air and land war lay behind the policy of dislocating surface communications on the mainland of Europe prior to D-Day. The policy was worked out by Zuckerman, who had made a close study of the effects of air bombing. During the advance of the Allied Forces into Sicily, and up the length of Italy, he had noted the great difference in effectiveness between uncoordinated strikes at railway communications and the planned and methodical dislocation of the nodal points of the enemy communication system. With the first policy, the damage was all too often quickly repaired. Properly executed, he argued, the second could create such inefficiency that ultimately chaos would spread like a creeping paralysis throughout the system. He and his staff estimated that if it were applied to the railway systems of northern Europe, such a form of strategic dislocation could delay the passage of some nine German divisions to the D-Day beach-heads by at least a week. The arguments were accepted some three months before the invasion, and the policy put into effect. It soon caused widespread breakdown of industry in the affected regions. As for the military effects, an official history records that 'sufficient evidence had been gathered from enemy sources of the delayed arrival of certain enemy divisions in the battle area to justify Professor Zuckerman's and the railway experts' contentions . . . it is a striking case where scientific advice had a profound influence on the conduct of military operations'.

With the end of the war, there were no more events to observe. But military technology went on changing, to such an extent that military staffs soon found themselves planning for a potential strategic conflict that, as time went on, lay increasingly outside their direct personal experience. This remains true today. None of the 'brush-fire wars' that have taken place since Korea, not even Vietnam, tells us anything about large-scale conflict between major powers. Since direct experience is now so hard to come by, military operational research into strategic conflict has perforce become much more a matter of prediction than of the analysis of past events; and a number of approaches have been evolved to make this task more tractable.

War-games, for example, have developed far beyond the old sand table into a sophisticated and (so far as possible) objective method of measuring the likely performance of a military formation under battle conditions. The actions of both sides are conducted according to a so-called 'rule book'—best thought of as a condensed summary of the most up-to-date military knowledge, couched wherever possible in numerical form. It specifies such things as ranges, hit probabilities, and rates of advance in various circumstances. Armed with these rules, the two sides play out engagements in which the course of events is determined by the probabilities set down in the rule book, so as to introduce the real-life element of chance. Of course, a fairly large number of replays will be necessary to obtain an idea of how far tactics or the effects of chance are influencing the outcome. But eventually there emerges a feeling for the capabilities of a new weapon in tactical situations. The war-gaming technique is slow and expensive in manpower; but it sharpens the intuition of the players, and provides something of a substitute for direct military experience.

The war-game in this form was painstakingly developed over many years by the former Army Operational Research Establishment at Byfleet. Its most important contribution to British military thinking has probably been in relation to the study of tactical nuclear war in Europe. Around 1960 there was much speculation on what kind of a conflict might take place if the state of mutual deterrence between N.A.T.O. and the Warsaw Pact countries were ever to break down. The importance of the Establishment's work was in bringing out difficulties in using tactical nuclear weapons: well-disposed and well-equipped military forces have a degree of protection, but civilians and civil facilities are both absolutely and relatively very exposed. Nowadays this conclusion seems almost self-evident. But the value of the work was that, for the first time, it provided a rough numerical estimate of what might happen in such a conflict, and enabled something of the scale of what might happen to be grasped.

Manual war-games are time-consuming, so it was natural to see whether a more computerized technique could be used instead. Computer war-games can certainly be developed to deal with minor engagements, like tactical encounters between tanks and anti-tank weapons. They can also be probabilistic in nature rather than deterministic, and the rapidity of a computed solution makes it possible to carry out sufficient replays to test the reliability of a conclusion. But they are inevitably more stereotyped—the complexities are limited to those that the programmer happens to have foreseen. They do not sharpen the intuition so effectively as manual games. Moreover, the computing power available sometimes tends to outrun the quality of the basic input data, on which, of course, depends the success of the calculation.

Attempts have always been made by the military to replace the direct experience of war by observing what happens in field exercises, but in modern conditions the conclusions are not always easy to evaluate. For one thing, a good deal of the most important side of military policy making tends to centre round the capabilities of weapons that cannot possibly be in service for perhaps another decade. The weapon itself clearly cannot be available in time for the making of a decision. Nor, if it takes so long to develop, is it likely that any existing weapon will be capable of fully simulating its capabilities. And even if this were not so, ordinary military exercises are often too slow, and almost always too expensive in manpower, to be a feasible method of exploring anything like the desirable range of military options.

But since appeal to experiment has obvious attractions, the Byfleet establishment (now renamed the Defence Operation Analysis Establishment) has attempted to develop a technique in which the best features of modelling and of special field experiments (not conventional exercises) are combined. The method involves analysing the problem and separating those aspects that can be regarded as primarily a matter of probability (which can be studied on a computer) from those concerned with the physical performance of a man or machine (which must be measured in the field). The next step is to design an experiment—it need not take the form of a normal military exercise—to obtain input data for a computer model of a typical engagement. The final stage is to work through the model a number of times to test the robustness of a solution in a variety of typical situations. This method was adopted in a study of tactically optimal designs for night-fighting visual aids, where a balance had to be struck between the competing requirements of providing sufficient light amplification, while also ensuring a worthwhile field of view. The best balance was not intuitively obvious, but a combination of modelling and experiment provided a useful and clear-cut indication.

The higher the level of the problem, or the more numerous the events with which it is concerned, the less possible is it to generalize about the best approach. In any case, it may take weeks or months of hard work before the main issues can be seen clearly enough for the best approach to be selected. Thus a problem studied at Byfleet a few years ago, concerning the likely future value of the British commando ships, involved initially an enormous collection of data on likely situations; naval capabilities; capabilities of alternative ways of carrying out broadly similar military tasks; the costs of both the ships and of the various alternatives like air transport; and so on.

Throughout all this preliminary work the real intellectual difficulty lay in devising a method for comparing the value of alternative policies on a fair and objective basis. Neither the costs nor the effectiveness of the alternatives matched exactly, so that like could never be compared with like. There was also a formidable problem of marshalling the data. But eventually a major clarification stemmed from a realization that many of the issues involved were capable of being described in terms of an 'objective function', which determined the most economic method of meeting a given set of military requirements. The arithmetic was complicated: there were several hundred simultaneous constraints to be considered, and the whole analysis involved making use of no less than 10 000 pieces of numerical data. It was, in fact, the largest integer linear-programme problem that had been solved up to that time in Britain. But when it was finished it not only gave answers that were themselves a useful guide, but also showed how to relate expenditure on the three Services to military effectiveness (as measured by the rate of reaction or the weight of attack) in a situation that was far too complex for any reliable solution to be inferred by inspection of the problem.

In major studies of this kind it is important to keep one's feet on the ground. This is the purpose of *scenario analysis*. Coupled with the techniques of technological assessment—the prediction of the technical capabilities of a new piece of equipment—it enables a new device to be evaluated against a realistic operational background. In this way we can study, say, the most effective design of surface-to-air guided weapons for defending an air base. The term 'most effective' carries with it an unspoken qualification: within a reasonable cost. The problem is to decide at what level of cost and sophistication any further improvement of the specification becomes of only very marginal value. Starting from a realistic scenario we can work out in detail just what the probabilities of success for enemy and defenders might be in actual engagement. Naturally we cannot take account of accidents, or of extreme bravery or cowardice. But the calculation gives something to go on. It shows whether the defence of the base is a reasonable thing to ask of the defenders. And it provides some sort of rationale for tackling the perennial difficulty of the best being the enemy of the good.

There are of course hidden dangers—from 'over-egging the scenario' and so arriving at needlessly extravagant equipment policies, to taking so long over an analysis that the decision to commit development funds has to be taken on quite other grounds, and perhaps on too little information. The practitioners of management science, or operational analysis as it is called in the military field, are not court wizards, and are certainly not infallible. But their painstaking attempts to predict the consequences of a particular policy are of unquestionable value, just as the accompanying process of 'open explicit analysis'—to use one of Mr. Robert McNamara's favourite phrases—imposes a discipline during the approach march to a decision that, so far as anything can, provides some kind of insurance that the worst mistakes may have been avoided.

Civil management science

Application of management science to the field of civil government is a more recent growth. On the whole it is a more difficult field, with objectives that are hard to define unambiguously, or to separate from a host of qualitative or even political considerations. Defence has curiously few such problems: it creates its own philosophy, and its analysts can exercise their skills with only sideways glances at the rest of the world—at least until they come to questions of deterrence. Then they are wrestling with the problems of evaluating something that has no physical presence, but exists only in the mind.

Civil life is full of such concepts: the value of leisure, of time, of human life, of good health, of fresh air, of freedom from visual intrusion, of beauty, comfort, peace, and quiet. Analyses that gloss over these things are clearly deficient. Unfortunately, in most cases we do not know how to express them in numerical terms, and unless we can do so we are inhibited from using some of our most powerful mathematical techniques. So we are often forced to deal with something less than the whole problem—to 'sub-optimize'. Until we learn how to do better we must take care that at the end of an elaborate series of calculations we explicitly draw attention to the factors that we have not been able to include, and whose weight can be assessed only by the old-fashioned (but still very powerful) process of subjective human judgement.

The kind of problems that can already be tackled with a fair degree of success are exemplified by the studies carried out over the past two or three years in the Ministry of Transport. I shall give three examples, one dealing with a new port, another involving inter-urban roads, and the third concerned with the development of a major conurbation.

The first concerns the proposal for a new dock at Portbury, near Bristol. The object of the investigation was an independent cross-check of the estimates of traffic that might be attracted to the new dock, if it were built, this being the key factor influencing approval or rejection of the £30 million scheme. A relatively simple 'gravity-type' model—one where distance is the major variable—was developed to explain the major import and export commodity flows between ports and inland manufacturing and population centres. When applied to Portbury the model predicted levels of trade substantially lower than those quoted in support of the development. The scheme was therefore not proceeded with; and a precedent was created by the inclusion, in the White Paper presenting this conclusion to Parliament, of considerable mathematical justification for the decision.[1]

My second example concerns a study of the Morecambe Bay barrage project, which contained an option as to whether or not the barrage, if built, should carry a road at an additional cost of over £6 million. A traffic model of the movements in the area was built up, and projected the behaviour patterns into the future so as to give traffic-flow forecasts for various alternative road network options. The economic returns, using discounted cash flow techniques, and estimates of savings of time and distance and benefits to new traffic, were then used to rank various possible alternative methods of connecting the barrage to the main road network.

The third comes from the field of urban transport planning, where the problem of how to secure a workable balance between public and private transport is at its most difficult. The starting-point for the evaluation of alternative network options is nowadays normally a major traffic survey, followed by an attempt to model the results in such a way that they can be projected into the future. Traffic and transportation modelling, as a body of knowledge, evolved in the late 1950s, mainly in the United States. But by the late 1960s the essentially *ad hoc* nature of the model procedures was becoming evident from attempts to apply them to increasingly complex urban investment problems. Over the past three years the Ministry of Transport's Mathematical Advisory Unit has spent a good deal of effort in working over the ground, starting from fundamental principles. They employed a statistical-mechanics approach to model building. The aim was a self-consistent set of models and sub-models, sufficiently well correlated with the physical events being studied to permit valid extrapolations into the relatively long-term future, when the car population may well have doubled. This model-building work is now being tested in a real planning study of the Manchester conurbation. Alternatives involving an expenditure of £200 million on roads and public transport are being studied on a basis that is not only self-consistent, but also includes some of the inconvenience and loss-of-time factors that real-life travellers take into account when choosing just how or whether to make a journey.[2]

No one pretends that we are yet in a position to assess all the social effects of every new policy in numerical terms, and there will always be a need to apply the ordinary processes of judgement to those aspects of the matter that still lie outside the grasp of cost-benefit analysis and modelling. But it is nevertheless reasonable to hope that in time such aspects will form a smaller proportion of the total than at present. Certainly some progress is being made, and it is no longer always out of the question to attempt a description of the social as well as the operational and financial consequences of a transport investment proposal. For example, in the case of an urban motorway, we can describe the likely street occupancy along feeder routes, traffic genera-tion, time savings, and to some extent noise levels. Even this relatively limited list provides the top levels of management with a more detailed appreciation of some of the relevant factors than they could otherwise obtain.

In this way, management science is of direct value to decision-mak-ing. But the approach also brings to the surface, quite naturally, an awareness of gaps in our existing knowledge, particularly about the long-term effects of decisions taken today. When modelling a national road-building programme, we soon realize that the pro-gramme itself, if large enough, will substantially change the pattern of employment, of job location, and of land use; and that to do the job thoroughly we ought ideally to use techniques that will measure in some way whether the outcome will be 'better' than the starting-point. At the moment, we have no really convincing techniques for making just judgements. But at least an attempt at modelling, or 'gaming', will show what kinds of data ought to be collected now, in order to let us do better in ten years' time.

Everywhere we look in the civil sector of government we find similar problems of deciding how best to use existing resources, or how to allocate the money available for future investment. The problems may be tactical: the optimal replacement policy for a large fleet of vehicles; forecasts of car ownership; the rationalization of hospital groupings with a view to greater efficiency; management of air-traffic control. Or they may be strategic: modelling the energy sector of the economy; policy for the third London airport; urban motorway policy: pre-dicting the output and requirements of the educational system. We cannot afford everything, so must choose—between jam today and jam tomorrow: between jam here and none there. Wherever the choice involves prior research, or the balancing of trade-offs between one policy and another, or between immediate 'patch and mend' and something better in the longer term, there will be a job for the management scientist.

Organization

Let us now look briefly at the problems of fitting an analytical function of the kind I have sketched into the organization of a large department. For problems at the tactical level, whose study can be regarded as an obviously useful on-demand service to the rest of the department, there is very little difficulty—though the analytical group must be big enough to embrace sufficient diversity of experience and guarantee sufficient debate during the study process. The big central issues round which the main work of a large nationalized industry or a government department revolve are another matter. Since a department's *raison d'être* is the settling of policy in relation to just such issues, it is obvious that the incorporation of a new group—indeed a new type of group—could have a major effect on the conduct of business. Badly handled, it could create stresses which, in difficult work where objectivity is a prime requirement, are far from desirable. Most management consultants know of cases in large organizations where something of this kind has happened.

The choice lies, in essence, between an independent group of assessors reporting directly to the head of the department—or at least at a very high level—and something altogether more closely integrated into the fabric of the organization. The former pattern was adopted by Mr. McNamara during his administration of the Pentagon. It has also existed in an even more independent form in the French Ministry of Defence.

In Britain, however, the tendency has been rather in the reverse direction, not only in the Civil Service, but also in large corporations where problems on a similar scale have to be tackled. These differences reflect the underlying differences in the pattern of public administration, and thus indirectly in the national temperament. We are not a presidency and, on the whole, the idea of a small 'cabinet' of privileged advisers, reporting separately from the rest of the system, is alien to our way of doing business. With our long Civil Service traditions we prefer a more organic approach, believing that in the long run it will make for a more healthy departmental structure. A price has to be paid, of course, in the time spent in consultation with colleagues, and the extra care in ensuring that consultation does not erode the independence of the judgements reached by the analytical unit. But this is a small price to pay for the benefits of an atmosphere of mutual confidence.

Take, for example, the code of practice governing studies carried out within the British Ministry of Defence. The terms of reference of each major study are carefully laid down, in writing, and agreed with the sponsoring division or department. Usually this stage is not completed until some weeks of preliminary study have elapsed, during which a problem that originally may have been stated in very general terms—e.g. what is the value of the Commando ships?—has been recast into what might be called a researchable form. This is usually a most fruitful period, for it is when the hard thinking on the relevance of external factors is done. It may also be necessary to persuade the client or sponsor that the problem cannot be tackled satisfactorily without giving more time, or going a good deal wider than had originally been anticipated.

Problems multiply if the 'researchable' form involves the study of organizations other than the original sponsors, as it may well do if there are a number of possible ways of achieving a particular end, or of substituting a new method for one that has traditionally been employed in the past. All these problems have to be set out and cleared with those who will later provide the basic information, if the study is not to run on the rocks.

Although they take care to speak publicly with a single voice, government departments are far from being the monolithic organizations they may appear to be when conducting their ordinary day-to-day work. Like any other large institution, they are made up of individuals and professional groupings, often with strongly held views. They cannot be otherwise if the process of debate, out of which mature judgement is born, is not to atrophy. In one important respect, these professional groupings within government are like those found anywhere else: they are sometimes a little reluctant to pass on information when they are not clear about the uses to which it will be put—particularly if their own future is likely to be affected.

A management-science organization cannot survive without reliable information. So the only workable course is to allow, indeed to encourage, any organization providing information, or likely to consider itself affected by a study, to contribute observers or participants. This is always done in the Ministry of Defence studies. These observers have the right, and the duty, to keep their principals informed of progress. In return, the study team is assured of easy access to a very wide range of information, of the kind that only close co-operation at a human and personal level is ever likely to dig out of the files. Moreover, the report is shown in draft to those who have contributed information, and to those likely to be affected by the findings, before being formally published or sent to the sponsor. And, finally, the report is advisory. Whether or not to take action is not for the analysts to decide.

It may sound a cumbersome procedure; perhaps at times it is. But it works reasonably well, and is itself something that conduces to a higher standard of analysis than might otherwise be the case. The need for some such procedure is in any case not confined to defence. The same need for consultation can be discerned wherever a major national issue is being studied—the third London airport, or the London ringway system are obvious examples—although in such cases the sheer mechanics of consultation make it that much more difficult to set up a procedure that will satisfy everybody.

To sum up: management science can undoubtedly make a significant contribution at almost all levels of policy making, and over a very wide range of subjects. It is strongest when dealing with factors that can be expressed in numerical form, when the power of mathematical and computer techniques can open the way to sophisticated cost-benefit calculations, precise estimates of the value of trade-offs between alternative policies, and other useful indicators that the ordinary descriptive processes of administration would have difficulty in providing. But there are definite limits to its powers. The management scientist is hampered if he cannot deal in facts that can be expressed numerically. And his attempts at striking a qualitative balance will often have to be reinforced by political and social judgements of the kind that public administrators have been used to making for centuries. Partnership, properly arranged, between the old methods and the new is likely to yield the best results.

The great opportunity offered by management science is the creation of a bridge between the two professions, which have been driven apart during the last hundred years by increasing specialization. A growing number of scientists will now cross this bridge. The profession of public administration is bound to be enriched by the recruitment of men who understand, from having done some pioneering themselves, when to turn to science; and—just as important—where its limitations lie.

References

1. *Portbury: Reasons for the Minister's decision not to authorize the construction of a new dock at Portbury, Bristol.* H.M.S.O. (1966).
2. *Transportation research* **4**, no. 103 (1970).

Index

ALLISON, D., 45, 54
American Academy of Science, 7–8
atomic energy, 1–2, 10–11, 16–21, 26–7, 55–6
Atomic Energy Research Establishment, *see* United Kingdom Atomic Energy Authority

BAKER, Sir JOHN, 38
BLACKETT of CHELSEA, Lord (P. M. S. BLACKETT), 83, 85
Bristol, *see* Portbury
British Research and Development Corporation, proposed, 4–5, 8
BROOKS, H., 7
business group, research in, 29–31
Byfleet, *see* Defence Operation Analysis Establishment

Capenhurst laboratory, 10, 11, 20
capital goods, 39
CASIMIR, H. B. G., 45–6
Central Advisory Council for Science and Technology, 57–8, 70
chemistry research, 32–7, 56
COCKCROFT, Sir JOHN, 9, 18, 55
consumer goods, 39
cost–benefit analysis, 25
creative environment, 44–8
creativity, and central laboratory, 28–37

DAVIES, D. S., 2, 13, 28–37
decision-making, 92–3
Defence Operation Analysis Establishment, Byfleet, 88
defence research and development, 5–6, 71–81
  aims, 78
  economics, 75–7
  establishments, 79–81
  organization, 77

design–production interface, 48–9
development department, organization, 2, 38–40, 93–6
displacement technique, 25

econometrics, 6
education
  and innovation, 2, 28–9, 41–2
  and labour relations, 29–30
engineering design and production, 3, 4, 5, 19, 38, 39, 40–2, 43–4, 48–54
engineering education, 41–2

FERRANTI, Sir VINCENT, 46–7
FISHLOCK, D., 1–8, 15
FLOWERS, Sir BRIAN, 9–12

GALBRAITH, J. K., 29
government, and management science, 82–96
Great Britain
  economy, 38–40, 42–4, 60
  industrial role, 39–40

HANSON, D., 23–4
Harwell, 10, 17–19
  industrial research, 3–4, 55–70, *see also* United Kingdom Atomic Energy Authority
HINSHELWOOD, Sir CYRIL, 29
HINTON, Sir CHRISTOPHER, 11, 19
HOLST, G., 45–6, 54

ideas, synthesis, 38–54
invention and innovation, 28–9, 31–2, 40–1

JANTSCH, E., 28
JEWKES, J., 54

KRONBERGER, HANS, 1–2, 9–12
KURTI, N., 10

laboratory, central, 2, 28–37
  for chemical industry, 32–7
logic, applied, 28, 29, 30–1
LONDON, H., 10

management science, 6–7
  and government, 82–96
  civil, 90–3
  military, 85–90
  organization of, 93–6
Manchester, 91–2
MARSHALL, W. C., 3, 14, 55–70
'maximum unfairness' principle, 4,
  67–8
Morecambe Bay barrage project, 91

National Research Development Corporation, 4
National Science Foundation (U.S.A.),
  8
nuclear power, 17, 18, 20, 26–7, 55–6,
  57

operational analysis, 84–90
operational research, 6, 83, 84, 85–6
organization, departmental, 38–40,
  93–6
Organization for Economic Development and Cooperation, 71, 72, 73,
  81
OWEN, Sir LEONARD, 11, 19

PILKINGTON, Sir ALASTAIR, 40
policy-making, 84
Portbury, 90–1, 96
POUT, H. W., 5–6, 14, 71–81
PRICE, B. T., 6–7, 14–15, 82–96
'principle of maximum unfairness', 4,
  67–8
problem-solving, 84–93
product development, 40–1, 48–54
production engineer, 52–3
project control and management, 20–3
project research and development,
  19–20

R and D, *see* research and development
Radio-Chemical Centre, Amersham,
  55
reactor development, 20, 26–7
Research Associations, 58, 62

research attitude, 30
research and development (R and D),
  1–2, 6, 8, 19–20
  conditions and environment for,
  44–54
  defence, 5–6, 71–81
  expenditure, national, 1, 71–4
  in business group, 29–31
  outside business group, 31–2
  national role, 74–5
  organization of, 1–3, 45–8
  project, 19–20
research staff, 23–4
resource allocation, 92–3
ROTHERHAM, L., 19, 20
Route 128, 42

SAWERS, D., 54
service departments, 53
SIMON, Sir FRANCIS, 10
size, effect on management, 45
social science, 7
sponsored research, 4, 57–70
STILLERMAN, R., 54
systems analysis and engineering, 6,
  49–50, 53–4

technological assessment, 7–8, 78
training, deficiencies in, 41
Transport, Ministry of, 84, 90–2

United Kingdom Atomic Energy
  Authority, 18, 20–3, 46, 55–70
  Culham laboratory, 56
  Industrial Group, 11, 19, 20, 25, 27
  industrial research, 58–70
  management organization, 19–27
  materials R and D, 56
  project R and D, 19–20
  project control, 20–3
  R and D branch, 19, 20
United States of America, 4–5, 7–8,
  38–9, 42, 43

war-games, 86–7
WHITFIELD, P. R., 50, 54
WILLIAMS, B. R., 73, 81
WILLIAMSON, D. T. N., 2–3, 13–14,
  38–54

ZUCKERMANN, Sir SOLLY, 83, 85–6